NEVER GIVE UP
ON YOUR MARRIAGE
UNTIL...

Author: S.R. Sutherland

Illustrator: Russell Tudor
Editor: Julia Houston
Chief Editor: Marc Baldwin
Publisher: stematsud

ISBN: 0615688160
ISBN-13: 978-0615688169
Library of Congress Control Number: 2012948469
Stematsud, Highland, CA

PREFACE

Dear Reader,

I want to remind you of how God's sacred institution of marriage is still woefully misunderstood by many. In so doing they have made several mistakes that could easily be corrected, rather than ruin their marriages through lack of comprehension.

This book is based on a true story and intended to encourage those who are struggling with forces in their marriage as well as to inspire those who have decided to continue the journey.

Most of the names have been changed for the privacy of the individuals, and the names of certain places are also fictitious.

May all who read the following pages be blessed and comforted.

Dedicated to Matthew and his parents.

ACKNOWLEDGEMENT

Special thanks to my mother, whose support knew no limit. She could never be repaid for her time, which was offered selflessly.

To my stepmom and dad, thanks so much for being there when I needed you most as well as for listening when all I wanted to do was talk.

To the many family members and friends whose encouragement was priceless, I offer a sincere thanks to you as well. To my work supervisor, a profound thanks for her understanding. My beloved son Matthew a special thanks to him for being extremely patient with my constant typing as he was deprived of some of the attention that was rightfully his. Most of all, my gratitude to the Lord for his sustenance and omnipresence.

TABLE OF CONTENTS

CHAPTER 1:
THE MEETING

I t was an arrangement, and she was excited. She travelled for two hours from the clean, quiet residential town of Mandeville in Jamaica to Portmore, St. Catherine to meet "him" for the first time in church. Her mother Dims took the trip with her.

She was so nervous, but excited as she stopped by her aunt Lorraine's home in Portmore just ten minutes away from the church. She had been visiting Aunt Lorraine's house for the past twenty-six years, but that morning her heart was racing with expectation.

He did not know it, but she knew the meeting about to happen wasn't an accident.

She had heard about him and saw pictures at Aunt Lorraine's house about six months before, but at that time neither of them suspected he would ever come for a trip as he lived thousands of miles away in California.

He had immigrated to the United States at the early age of twelve and never returned to his native land. His dad, Godfrey, lived just five minutes down the street from Aunt Lorraine. He was always bragging about his boy and dreaming of the day he would return. Their parents got divorced, and he and his brother, nine at the time, had immigrated to America to be with their mom.

One unexpected day, Aunt Lorraine said that Godfrey had stopped at her house, and something had been very different about him. His expression was unreadable. He laughed, and then he cried. Without a doubt she was confused.

He slowly said, "Lorraine, can you believe that after all these years as I worried about my boy and you used to encourage me that one day he would return, he is coming to visit? He will be arriving in two weeks!"

Aunt Lorraine called Roberta, quite ecstatic, and told her that same afternoon that the young man she had seen in the photograph would be visiting in only two weeks. Roberta's response, however, was lukewarm.

Roberta remembered thinking that the guy in the picture had looked like a nice fellow and possibly a good prospect. However, she still had not gotten over the handsome young physician that she had been dating for two years. The thing was that although they had dated for so long, they did not share the same views about religion, and that bothered her immensely.

Aunt Lorraine told her that there was going to be a huge celebration at her church in Portmore that would coincide with Aubyn's trip. Actually, the church celebration would be three weeks after his arrival. She already told Godfrey that she would be extending an invitation to his son for the church celebration. Roberta decided she would attend the church service because meeting this young man would surely be harmless.

Godfrey was quite an expressive man, well-spoken and not reserved. Roberta remembered meeting him on one of her visits to her aunt's house and distinctly recalled the strange conversation.

The meeting had been rather unusual because he had heard Aunt Lorraine speak often of her niece but had never met her. On that visit,

Godfrey took one look at her and said, "Look at my daughter-in-law. Look at her. She would be a perfect fit for Aubyn."

She had been appalled, but being a respectful, reserved young woman, she kept the worst of her thoughts to herself. He appeared to be a man of great integrity, and of course she did not want to appear rude.

Her response was, "Aunty Lorraine speaks of you quite a bit, and although I have been here several times before I never had the pleasure of meeting you before, so I am truly delighted to meet you."

She knew he lived just five minutes down the street from her aunt's house. Whenever she came to visit her aunt and uncle as a child, Roberta, her brother, and her cousin Gary played close to that house. Except for the four huge German shepherds that prowled the balcony of the house, she had never met the occupants.

Gary told them that two kids lived there, but they played indoors, and their dad was extremely strict. She still could see the dogs vividly. The stately, intimidating creatures barked loudly as they passed by. The house stood out. It was the only one on the street with such a gorgeous balcony.

As she was jolted to reality, Roberta hoped Godfrey would be leaving soon. As she pondered his words she apparently succeeded in hiding her distaste. Why would he say such a thing? He was only meeting her for the first time, his son had not returned since age twelve, and he must have been at least in his late twenties by now. Was this a premonition?

After all, he did not really know her. He did not know that she had a boyfriend, her first-ever special friend, and she believed that they would get married at some point. He was her one and only love. He was a handsome young physician, she a pharmacist. They worked at the same hospital and both lived in Mandeville. How strange was the comment. He had to be a crazy man!

So Roberta and her mom drove from the house with Aunt Lorraine and her husband, Uncle Lou, driving their car close behind.

Roberta entered the church with trepidation as she felt like Aubyn's eyes were piercing her in the huge church even though she did not even know if he were already there.

She entered through the right side door of the church, and the racing of her heart would not stop. Oh, how she wished it would. By now it was 9:15 am, and the song service had just begun. She knew Aunt Lorraine normally sat at the third bench on the right side of the church, so she made her way there with Dims. Her aunt and uncle followed suit.

Her eyes searched for Aubyn, but none of the faces so far looked like the picture she had seen. She started to feel dismay. Maybe he was not coming to the service after all. Knowing Aunt Lorraine, the perfect matchmaker, she would have given him the specifics as to the seating. By the time she was through with the details he would not be able to miss it.

Roberta saw in her peripheral vision that Aunt Lorraine rose from her seat. She left for a while and—oh my, oh no, oh yes—she did not return to her seat alone. Accompanying her were three other persons: two fine young men and a classy-looking middle-aged lady.

Her heart must have been popping out her chest because she felt the throbbing. She felt hot and flushed all over. Aubyn was definitely there, and the young man next to him bearing some resemblance must be his brother, and definitely the lady was his mother.

The service was well underway, and the church was filled. In the midst of it all, Aunt Lorraine stretched over her husband and said, "Roberta this is Aubyn, his brother Dean, and his mom Phena."

Reserved, quiet, and quite shy, she responded, "It is nice to meet you. I am Roberta." She would just die if they ever knew that this was all planned, they did not just happen to be invited by her aunt, and she did not just stumble upon them.

Church at Portmore was normally great, and she was sure it was great on that day as well, but she was not really listening as her anticipation arose. She couldn't help wondering how the rest of the day would unfold knowing her aunt Lorraine.

Church finally ended. The drive home was carefully orchestrated by Aunt Lorraine, of course, and poor Roberta would soon learn that Uncle Lou was as much a matchmaker as his wife, if not more so.

Roberta was told that Aubyn would sit in the front seat next to her as she drove to her aunt and uncle's place for lunch. Phena and Dims would ride in the back. Aunt Lorraine and Uncle Lou would transport Dean and their children home.

Roberta arrived at the house first. As she drove into the garage, the others pulled in afterward. She was about to see the handiwork of her relatives.

Her aunt and uncle entered the house with everyone filing in behind. They were led to the dining room, which Roberta thought was amazing.

The table that normally sat eight was made to seat all nine. It was elegantly spread with a crisp white table cloth and trimmed with a wine red color. The array of dishes was exquisite. There were eight dishes to choose from. The tropical fruits such as nase berries, plums, melons, pomegranates, guavas, and mangoes looked absolutely mouthwatering.

Uncle Lou, a normally quiet man with very few words, had seemingly limitless energy. As he jumped around ensuring that everyone was having their fill and well entertained, he said with delight, "I am a man with a mission."

Aubyn was at the head of the line as all made their way along the table arranged buffet-style. Dims noticed that Aubyn appeared a bit timid as he helped himself to the meal. Dims smiled and took his plate, and as she began to pile portions of each available kind of food on it, he responded with a grin, "Load it on."

The meal was great. It was tasty and filling, but Roberta did not eat much. She felt like a bundle of nerves, and it was exciting.

After the meal some settled in the living room while others gathered on the front patio. Dims and Phena were chatting away, and ever so often there were outbursts of laughter. They talked as though they were old friends.

At one point, Phena said, "I am a Gemini, born June 1st.

Dims said, "Oh, that's why we get along so well. I am a Gemini also, born June 5th." Then they laughed harder.

Phena showed no end of interest in Roberta. "She is a lovely young lady, and I am looking for a good gal for my boy," she said.

Dims instantly loved this woman and thought she had to be an answer from God. Both women started to talk eagerly about their children.

It was so much more intriguing when the two realized that their kids had birthdays just a day apart! Aubyn's was February 24, and Roberta's was the day before. This had to be a match made in heaven, they thought, surely a divine plan. As they talked they realized that both their kids had so much more in common. They even had several of their teeth removed prior to being fitted with braces to correct their extreme overbite. Both women laughed as they chatted away. It was too good to be true.

Dean was quite at home talking with everyone, including the children and the "man with a mission" and his wife. Aubyn and Roberta were seated by themselves at one end of the front porch overlooking the mango trees and the gorgeous hibiscus and roses. They seemed to be enjoying each other's company.

They talked about how he left the island of Jamaica and only returned now after fifteen years for a family reunion. He said he and his brother communicated with their dad through letters and telephone calls. He had a very mature outlook on life about wanting to achieve many things before he took a trip back.

The conversation appeared very light for a while, and as they grew more comfortable together he asked, "Are you attached?" She was very surprised because he was reserved and quite the gentleman. She was feeling a racing of her heart and great delight.

She answered, "Well, not exactly."

He was a little quiet as he apparently pondered her words, then he asked again, "So, are you attached?"

She tried to explain that she was with a fellow, the first boyfriend she had ever had, but they had been on and off in their friendship. She wanted to tell him that the relationship was frustrating as their beliefs and views are desperately different, but it was too early to divulge so much.

She also wanted to tell him that she was hoping that this was the "refreshing" break she dreamt of.

As it became dark, Aubyn's dad from down the street dropped by the house and suggested that they take a ride up the hill to Smokey Vale where his uncle's house was. Roberta pondered the invitation then said, "Yes, why not? Sounds like fun."

In a little while Roberta's cousin Gary came by with his sixteen-seat van, and up the hill they went. It was exhilarating and just thrilling to take that ride knowing she would spend a little more time with Aubyn. He was really nice to be around.

They all loaded up into the van, Aubyn, Roberta, Aubyn's mom, his dad, Dean, and Gary. Gary was one of those macho kind of guys who liked fast driving and turning the simplest moment into a thrill.

As they were on their way to Smokey Vale, Roberta thought it was an awesome sight. Although the road was winding and extremely narrow with absolutely no passing lane, the air was cool and clean. At 6,000 feet they were overlooking the beautiful city of Kingston.

Gary kept swerving in and out and out and in again, and they felt they were too close to that treacherous ravine. Aubyn's mom, who seemed to be quite the talker, was the most scared of all. She screamed, "Please, let us head back down the hill! I want to live to return to California." But in spite of Gary's seeming to enjoy giving the group a scare, he was a careful driver.

When they finally reached the top, Roberta was glad she decided to take the trip. The view was unbelievably beautiful. As Roberta disembarked, she saw huge houses with such intricate designs and exquisite architecture. His Uncle Henry's house was by no means any different.

Everyone was just awestruck at the outside and wondered what must be on the inside. Uncle Henry, his wife Lonnie, and two of the grounds men gave a quick briefing of the area. They were amazed to learn that at least three celebrities lived just few houses away.

Uncle Henry's house was very large, three stories high and boasting seven bedrooms with a balcony on the outside of each. As they entered the house they passed by a huge kitchen with two helpers preparing the evening meal. The setting was undeniably looking like a five star hotel.

There was a formal living room that seemed unused, then a much larger family room that must have been the common room in which everyone hung out.

Aubyn jokingly said to Roberta, "You know what? While everyone is captivated by all this, I want us to chat a while longer. You return to Mandeville tomorrow, although I still have a week left out here. I am pretty sure this is it for us."

The disappointment that overtook her was painful. She then chided herself, *You only met this young man a few hours ago. What did you think it was going to be? Well, this certainly is a weekend with a difference. At least I had some fun.*

They picked a cozy spot in a den on the second floor overlooking the pool. They sat close, talking about the events that day and enjoying the view. The city was so beautiful to look at with all those lights. Just before it had gotten dark they had spotted Palisadoes Airport in the distance. It was just beautiful enjoying the scenery and sitting close.

Roberta was getting very conscious of the time. "I better go check on Gary because once there is food and entertainment time is of no consequence to him."

True to the word, she found him seated on the ground floor across from the gym. He was surrounded by a plate of jerked chicken, at least a dozen delicious-looking fried golden cornmeal festivals, a glass of sparkling grape juice, and a bowl of fruit.

Totally sprawled in front of the huge fifty-inch television with remote in hand, he asked, "Cousin, have you guys gone for a swim yet?"

She just told him sweetly, "You might not be aware of it, but it's now 9:30 pm, and we have a long way down this hill, and may I remind you no goofing around down those winding road."

It was time to put an end to a special day. Roberta was not sure why she thought "special day," but in spite of the meaning of this meeting, if there were even a meaning, she felt content to mark it as such.

The parting was longer than she wanted it to be.

The trip from Smokey Vale would be a quiet one, consisting only of Roberta, Godfrey, and Gary, as the rest of the crew were staying over at Uncle Henry's.

Phena trumped up a conversation that was definitely premature. She asked Roberta, "So do you have a visa to visit the States?"

"Yes, I do."

"Good then. So when do you plan to take a trip?"

Honestly Roberta could not believe she could be so direct. She was even more astounded when Phena asked, "Would you live in the States?"

Roberta's answer shocked her as she said, "I do not want to live anywhere but here. This is my home. This is where my family is."

Very bold, Phena said, "Well, that's going to be a problem."

Aubyn spoke up quietly. "Mom, why all these questions? It does not matter. There is always the telephone."

It felt awkward, and the parting was not the way it should have been as they said their good-byes. She thought this might be the last time she saw this man.

Sunday morning came fast. Roberta woke up early as she got her things together, and she and her mother headed down to Mandeville on their two-hour ride home. They were going back to reality. There would be no fairy tale in this life.

Monday morning would see her back to work at the hospital pharmacy and her mother back to teaching, a job she had held for over thirty years.

CHAPTER 2:
THE PARTING

Monday morning was a typical one. Roberta got dressed and headed off to work, where everything was normal. The only thing was that she kept reflecting on yesterday. She kept checking her email, but found nothing, at least nothing from him. He did not call all day either.

Well, he knows I'm at work, so that must be the reason.

The disappointment was overwhelming, especially living alone in her apartment with her thoughts as her companion. She had dinner as usual then sat by the television for the evening news. The telephone rang, and she jumped to get it with a vibrant hello. It was not him. She just decided, *You know what? That was yesterday. It was just a meeting. Nothing special. Forget that. Get back to your routine.*

Just as she was about to have a shower, the phone rang again. She approached without anticipation, and this time it was her mom wanting to chat.

Roberta had to work the next morning as usual, so she decided she might as well get dressed for bed.

She checked her phone one last time and found there were two missed calls and two voicemails, duplicates of each other from Aubyn.

"Looks like I wrote the wrong house number. I called at least three times, and I kept getting a strange recording, so I decided to try your cell. If you receive this message, please call me, and I will call right back."

He did call, and they had a good chat. He had six days to return to the United States and guaranteed that every evening for the remaining days they would talk to each other. The romance began over the telephone. They knew they would not be seeing each other again for a very long time, but they knew they definitely wanted to someday.

As the days went by, he shared with her that he had waited this long to return home to the Caribbean and had no immediate plans to return. She knew she wanted to visit at some point, but he also would need to do the same.

Aubyn started to express deep regret. "Roberta, I am sorry we did not even share a kiss. Now I have nothing to take away with me except the feel of your hands and the look on your face.

That was a problem. Things started to become serious over the phone, and emotions are now quite involved. Would she be required to immigrate someday? She knew he was not going to be relocating to the land she loved so much as he was more a Californian than anything else. She saw serious problems, and this truly concerned her.

Aubyn called that Friday afternoon to say his good-bye, and she imagined that she could see Phena, Dean, and her dear Aubyn board the plane. She cried as though she were at the airport and was seeing the plane lift off and fly out of sight.

He wasted no time. The following day he emailed her that his return trip went well and assured her that he would be keeping in contact very frequently.

Days went by, and her life no longer felt the same. In just one day of meeting this gentleman her world had been transformed. Clint called as usual, but she no longer looked forward to those calls. His calls were infrequent anyway, so she was not missing much. They already knew that there were issues and no clear way forward.

She could not call Aubyn frequently as overseas calls were expensive, plus the time difference of three hours was such an inconvenience. He, also being a cautious spender, did not call straight from his land line or mobile phone, but he was going through phone cards rapidly. It was really becoming costly.

They tried to work around the time difference. She was told that in the States time "springs" forward during the spring time and "falls" back during fall, while in her country they operated off standard time. Since the time in Jamaica did not change irrespective of the season there would be times when the time difference between them would be two hours rather than three. She was looking forward to that.

Roberta heard from a friend about a device that utilized either the telephone line or voice-over Internet. Since she didn't own a computer she would opt for the former. It would cost a few thousand dollars in her currency, about US$100, which was quite expensive for her. She thought the investment would be worth it, however, as the rate was only a few cents per minute. The hardest part was purchasing the device.

She made the purchase thinking that at the rate at which she wanted to talk with Aubyn it definitely would be cost-effective. It worked beautifully. The sound was clear, the delay was not very noticeable, and it felt great. Every day they talked. Either he would call or she would.

Approximately six weeks after buying the device, she ran to the phone after getting in from work and performing her usual routine. The device was not working. She unplugged it. She tried troubleshooting as far as her technical skills would permit. Nothing.

Tears were in her eyes. She tried to squeeze them back, but they just came pouring out as she asked herself why. She thought of what it had cost her and the sacrifice she had made to get it. It hurt more than ever that she would no longer have the freedom to call him whenever she felt like it. At least that way he did not feel so far away. Although he called at least every other day, she did not want to sit around waiting for his call. It just was not the same.

She talked with the friend who initially told her about it, but he was clueless regarding its functionality. Roberta took it back to the shop where she purchased it and was basically told that she was stuck with it and that there was no warranty.

Aubyn was getting frustrated too. "You know, sweetie," he said. "If you had access to a computer we could email each other and chat online. There are also some neat programs that would provide us the opportunity to talk to each other. Besides, the quality is pretty good."

She has always been quite independent. She would never ask a guy for anything, but she wondered if he would offer a computer. She knew she could not afford one any time soon. In her currency it would cost her at least $50,000. If he made her an offer she was not going to refuse, she thought. After all, it would be a gift for them both. She tried convincing herself. *It's not like I was asking him for it.* She then chided herself for jumping the gun. *He did not even say he was getting you one.*

She was not able to call him, and she realized he was calling less and less. Was it worth it, she wondered? Did this make any sense? Surely this was a sign from God that this was not working.

Her thoughts started straying. Clint did say he wanted to see her. After all, she had known him over two years, and she had barely known Aubyn four months. Whatever the challenges or doubts were with Clint, at least she knew him a lot better, and he was right there.

One day she realized she had not heard from Aubyn in four long days. Her sadness and disappointment could not be greater, she thought. She wondered why he was not calling her. It was not her fault that this thing stopped working. Didn't he believe her? Did he think she was making excuses not to speak with him? Or worse, maybe he had returned to some special lady friend that he did not bother to mention. He did not say he was involved, but could he be and has been concealing it.

Roberta worked Monday to Friday and alternate Sundays. One Sunday she was off from work, and Roberta enjoyed getting an early start when she had chores so she could relax the rest of the day.

She arose earlier than usual at 7:45 am and started off by cleaning her bathroom. She mopped her two-bedroom apartment, and then she tackled the laundry. She felt like she was getting things accomplished. Just one last task, she decided, as she really was getting tired. It was back to work tomorrow, so she would cook enough dinner to have some to fix for lunch the next day.

She baked chicken, made escoveitched fish, macaroni and cheese, potato salad, rice and red beans, and then she made a natural juice by blending melons, pineapples, and mangoes. It was a wonderful meal, but she had no one with whom to share it. She was through with everything just around 3 pm. She wanted to settle down to a nice meal, but decided to have a long bath first so she could truly enjoy dinner.

There was a knock on her door. She peeked through the door, and it was Clint. She thought with some irritation that he had not even bothered to call first. She had not seen him in over three months. But, she thought, at least she would have someone to share the meal with her.

He was on call at the hospital that night and for whatever reason decided to drop by. He surely ate quite a large plate and helped himself to a second. She too enjoyed the meal, but did not eat too much.

She really was happy for the company, but wanted to relax after her meal. He was in no hurry to leave. The hospital was less than ten minutes down the street if they needed him. She did not know how to tell him, but she hoped he would leave soon. She just wanted to relax undisturbed at this point.

His pager went off. *Saved by the bell*, she thought as Clint bent over to hug her and give her a kiss on the cheek. She heard when he dialed the hospital and was giving instructions about setting up the drip of lactated ringers to run at whatever the rate was per minute.

"I think this will be pretty quick," he told her. "I will pass by to see how things are going and go over the vitals. I figure I will be back before you know it."

However, he did not come back that evening, and she was relieved. Another day maybe, she thought, but not right now. It was funny how exhausted she felt, yet when the phone suddenly rang she felt a rush of energy. As she said hello, there was excitement.

She heard Aubyn's quiet voice say, "Hi, hon. Miss me?"

She wanted to say, "Of course, stupid," but she wanted to find out first what had happened: four days and nothing, not a single word.

"Roberta, I thought of calling you so many times, even yesterday, but the past few days I have been bombarded at work. I have been leaving after 9 pm, and by the time I got home it was closer to 10, undoubtedly too late for you. Wouldn't that be almost one in the morning over there?"

They tried to fill each other in on what had been going on. They must have been talking for close to an hour when he said, "Sweetie, I am sorry to keep you up. Poor thing, you need to get your rest." He talked so tenderly to her, such a soft voice, so unbelievably caring.

It always felt so special talking with him, but they both knew something was missing. How long would it be before they gazed at each other or held hands or shared a kiss? She would not complain. She had enough patience to wait. As long as she heard his voice frequently and exchanged thoughts she could get by, at least for now.

It was strange how things unfolded. Now that Roberta had a new interest in the person of Aubyn, Clint was calling her more than he ever did. She thought how much she would have welcomed this even four months ago. His interest in her seemed to spike, as though he knew that whatever it was they had was being threatened. There was no way he could know this because she had not told him yet. Besides, she did not think it really mattered because they were growing apart anyway.

Roberta was on a day off from work and had just gotten in after being out all day running errands. She packed in as much as she could in her days off as she got inside her apartment to find two messages from Clint. She had planned that she would be telling him the next time they spoke that their so-called friendship was going nowhere and they might as well quit now than later.

It was so unlike him: two messages in one day saying all the things she had always wished he would say. Why now? She did not need to be confused now. She was feeling like life had new meaning and direction. Why was he resurfacing in her life in such a marked way?

As she began playing the messages she wondered if she wanted to hear any more. "Girl, I want to see you, may I see you later? You haven't been calling any more. I am regretting that. I do long to hear your little voice on my answering machine."

The next message was a continuation. "This evening is your evening, no interruptions. Anything you want to do, anywhere you want to go. If you prefer tomorrow, say so. I will come running."

She smiled as he tried to sound like the singer as he borrowed those lines.

He came over the next day, and they laughed and talked just like it was when they first met. That had been Sunday, September 13, 1998. She never forgot because he was her very first. She remembered thinking when the first signs of trouble appeared that if it were not going to be him, she did not want anyone else and might as well be a nun.

Oh, how those days are long gone, she thought. Or were they fast returning?

She never had the guts to tell him about Aubyn. He showed up at her door casually dressed in jeans, a white polo shirt, and a baseball cap, and he was grinning in a carefree, mischievous way. He truly looked handsome, and those old feelings were coming back. She did not want to forget the problems they had, however, because he surely did change like a chameleon.

They went for a long ride to a place in Treasure Beach called Little Ochie. It was named after Ocho Rios, a beautiful area with several resorts and gorgeous beaches that tourist flocked to in the parish of St.Ann.

The fish and festival smelled great. As they made their way, they could see a fishing boat in the distance.

The jazzy music was relaxing and entertaining. Not too many people were there that Tuesday evening, so it was private and quiet. She ordered her meal first. The fish were freshly caught and laid out in the cooler. She needed to choose from the stack which one she wanted prepared. It was a difficult choice. There were parrot fish, snappers, goat fish, jack fish, and others she did not recognize.

She finally settled on a blue parrot fish. She ordered it steamed with fried bammies, a kind of cassava cake, and festival served up with carrots and herbs. The festivals were golden brown and made of cornmeal and flour with vanilla, sugar, and lots of mouth-watering spices.

Clint ordered a jack fish much larger than her own. The aroma, the music, and the company were fantastic. They laughed and talked as their order was being prepared. As their meals were served she wondered if she could manage to eat it all.

Clint said, "Gee, Robbey, it has been a long while since we spent time together like this. I had not realized how much I missed this, your company. Think we can do this more often?"

She was enjoying herself and wished life was not so complex. "Yeah, I guess so. I mean, for sure. It only depends on what's going on with work, and you know I always have something or other going on."

"Are you making excuses? I mean, if you need space and time I have that, for now, at least."

Roberta responded, "Oh, let's not go on getting all serious now. Let's enjoy the moment. It's so refreshing to feel so light and carefree right now."

They left Little Ochie around dusk. They could hear the pleasant peaceful sound of crickets as the evening grew darker. It was so tranquil and nice as they drove back, and she heard the waves rushing to shore in the darkness. The journey back home was about an hour long and was more quiet and reflective than anything else.

She got home, and the light mood immediately dissipated. He reached over and very softly said, "I had a wonderful evening. Thank you, and I hope you enjoyed it enough to come out again with me soon. I mean, take your time, but at least promise it will not be too long."

The old feelings of yearning and longing were coming back. After all, he was her very first boyfriend ever. How she would have welcomed this without reservation just few months ago. *Why is this happening now? Why when I just made up my mind we were going nowhere, and there appears so much promise in Aubyn?*

He kissed her on the mouth. She allowed it but did not respond. They said good-bye. He seemed happy, but her emotions were chaotic.

It was already 8:30. She was so full. It was just time to brush her teeth and get dressed for bed. She checked her phone as usual. There were no messages, but she saw that Aubyn had called. She had missed his call and was disappointed. She sighed, mentioned a prayer and drifted off to sleep.

CHAPTER 3:
HER VISIT TO HIS OVERSEAS HOME

Roberta was on two weeks' vacation. She had been planning to travel to the US in 2001 since her last trip had been three years earlier. It was her intention to visit her dad Gilford and stepmom Angela in Miami, but she changed her plans for California instead to see her dear Aubyn. Her dad and stepmom visited at least once a year so that was OK.

She had paid her fare two weeks prior. It was expensive because the airline told her it was peak season, and the return trip was US$800. She was the type of person to pay her bills and save the rest. She had a heart for helping others in need, but she still saved her pennies. At least with Air Jamaica she would not be changing planes. The flight was five and a half hours long, and she only had the hassle of claiming baggage once.

She did not realize that putting things together for the trip would be so time consuming. She was permitted two seventy-pound bags at no extra cost. She was planning to shop for herself and bring back few things for family and friends as she always did when she traveled abroad. She had lots of room to bring souvenirs for Aubyn and his family.

Her special souvenir spot was the Fontana pharmacy in Mandeville. Such beautiful craft work was there, creative designs all depicting the island and all made from materials readily available.

She got the feeling that Phena was very particular in taste, so she decided to find her gift first. Certainly they were not expecting her to bring them anything, but it was her nature to bring gifts when she traveled.

She found a beautiful salt and pepper shaker hand-carved from bamboo, and then as she walked through the aisle she saw a wooden napkin holder beautifully polished in dark brown. It was so beautiful she could tell it was made from good mahogany. There was also a painting of a guy rafting on the great Rio Minho River. She still had so many gifts to purchase and did not want to get both because they were not cheap.

She had difficulty deciding and just got both souvenirs instead. Aubyn's stepdad, from what she heard of him, did not want anything and was a man who did not care for such things. She got him a shirt from the island anyway depicting the legendary Bob Marley.

Dean seemed quite a particular gentleman also, but she could tell he would enjoy anything reminding him of the island and his trip there. She got him a beautiful baseball cap with the national colors: green, yellow, and black.

For Aubyn she bought a cute log-shaped keychain that was nicely polished in a natural wood color. She also got him a pen holder, mug, and wall plaque all with the island flavor. She was pleased with all of the gifts. Then she had the task of wrapping and packing in order to prevent any breakages.

It was Monday, December 31, 2001, three months after the sad day that she made the first trip over to visit Aubyn and his family. She felt a little apprehensive traveling by air because it was so soon after that awful day.

She embarked on the plane at 5 pm and braced herself for the long trip. The flight felt like forever, but at least she was not changing planes.

There were inflight movies, but she did not feel like watching one. She had a window seat and in between closing her eyes she looked outside and watched as it grew dark. She kept wondering what it would be like seeing him again, and her stomach felt hollow and strange.

The attendants served a meal two hours after takeoff. There was a choice between apple juice and fruit punch. The meal was stewed chicken with rice or stewed beef with rice. She did not eat beef, so she opted for the chicken and rice. It was good. They traveled for maybe another two hours, and the attendants came offering juice and snacks.

Soon after, the captain's voice announced, "We are cruising at 35,000 feet, and we should be arriving at LAX approximately one hour from now."

The rest of the trip seemed to speed by. The captain's voice was again heard over the intercom: "Ladies and gentlemen, please observe the seat belt warning. The temperature in LA is 56 degrees. We have started our descent, and we should be pulling into LAX momentarily. It was my pleasure serving as your captain, and I look forward to serving you in the near future."

As she disembarked and made her way through immigration then to the baggage claim area, the jittery feeling and trepidation were almost unbearable. She wanted to appear calm, confident, and composed when he saw her, and she feared that might not be the case.

She stepped outside after claiming her belongings, and the cold air hit her. It must have been at least 35 degrees because she felt close to freezing. She was only clad in a black jeans skirt and a long-sleeved red blouse, and she was still shivering especially her legs.

She looked around, and not one face looked like Aubyn. Her heart was sinking. She had expected to walk right out and see him waiting anxiously outside. She knew his mobile number, but she did not have a phone that worked overseas. She now regretted not putting the roving feature on her mobile phone, but she could not afford that extra expense.

It must have been more than twenty minutes that she stood waiting, tired and cold, not to mention disappointed. The crowd that she saw when she claimed her baggage gradually dwindled and just a handful remained. She saw a middle-aged gentleman, perhaps in his sixties, waiting just like herself. She walked towards him with determination. She thought she would ask him to allow her to make a quick telephone call if he had a phone with him. She needed to make contact with Aubyn somehow.

"Hi," she began. "It seems like we should have things switched around. I am waiting to be picked up, while you are waiting to pick up your visitor and there is no visitor." She smiled lightly, feeling perplexed, and wanted to cry.

The gentleman responded, "Yeah, but your accent sounds like an islander, and I am waiting for my nephew's friend that I have never met. You see, ever since the high security no more curbside parking is allowed at the airport, and so cars have to keep on moving. So my nephew left me to look out with a description of his friend and is now driving 'round and 'round. He claimed that he has been tracking the flight and there were no delays so there was no need for him to park."

He paused, looking at her, and then asked, "Could you be Roberta?"

They both laughed so hard they both felt ridiculous, but she was relieved. She thought it would be wiser for Aubyn to be looking out for her since he knew exactly whom he was waiting to see.

His uncle finally said, "I am Uncle Guy. He gave me such vivid description and said there was no way I should miss you."

Uncle Guy proceeded to tell her, "Man, he said, she is a petite little one, likes to wear knee-high skirts, and has really nice legs. I don't expect her to be wearing those little skirts tonight though. She has light brown complexion, a round face, bright eyes, and brown hair. Uncle Guy, there is no way you cannot spot her." Uncle Guy admitted that when he saw Roberta he still was unsure and didn't want to approach the wrong person.

As they stepped outside of the building and made their way to the pavement she saw a pretty greenish blue car pull up. She was not sure what make it was, but it looked like a Volvo that was common in her country. Quite a tough-looking but elegant machine.

There was no mistaking Aubyn. She saw what appeared to be all thirty-two teeth grinning as he approached the curb. He came out and gave her a shy but warm hug, then he patted his uncle on the back.

"Gee, Roberta, I am sorry, but Uncle Guy has been in there since 9:40, and your flight arrived 9:55 pm. I thought he would be able to figure out who you were." He shook his head twice and apologized repeatedly. "You poor thing, you must be so tired and hungry. Did you want to stop and grab a bite? There are several restaurants and food places around here." "No, but thanks. I'll be OK. I just would like to get home if you don't mind. Besides, the airlines served a meal and gave snacks during the flight."

"I'm not complaining, because heaven knows I like seeing you in those little skirts, but I thought you'd find the weather a bit nippy here considering your tropical climate. Aren't you cold?"

"My legs were just for a little bit, but I soon got used to it. It's really OK."

All this time Uncle Guy was quiet until he said, "Boy, congratulations man. Good eye. In my time it was birds like these I used to go for."

She did not quite like the term, but he did appear to be a fine uncle. After all, he had left his warm bed and traveled almost two hours to LAX to accompany his nephew.

"Thanks, Uncle. It's a family trait that we have good eye, eh?"

Aubyn's car was spacious and comfortable, and she could tell he was a careful driver. He was also very considerate. Although there were not many potholes, on a rare occasion when he eased into one he would say a quiet, "Sorry about that. I really tried to avoid that."

They drove for close to an hour and a half, and then it was time to drop Uncle Guy off at his home in Fontana. He was such good company that she missed him already.

Uncle Guy said, "Roberta, come say a quick hi to Anita. She is dying to see Aubyn's special friend. Just a quick hi and she will be happy."

In spite of being exhausted after the long six-hour flight and long drive to the airport, she said, "Sure, of course."

Anita had a very distinct accent. Roberta knew she was Asian, but was not sure of her precise ethnicity. She was a warm and soft-spoken lady. As she bent over and lightly hugged her and rested her face against Roberta's, she explained she already had some hot chocolate going with an irresistible-looking dark slice of cake with strawberries and cream on top. She ended up staying for close to thirty minutes.

Aubyn then got up and hugged his aunt and uncle. "I better get her home now. She is beat, I can tell, and she will not say so if I don't."

They said their good-byes and went back on the road. He told her that they were just thirty minutes away, and she was happy. She just wanted to have a quick warm shower and some sleep. The time difference made her even more exhausted because by the time they arrived at his mom's house in Raleigh Heights it was close to 1 am California time, but it already would be 4 am back on the island.

They pulled into his garage and entered the house. Of course, she could not see much, but it was a sprawling house. It was quiet everywhere, and she was glad because was she drained and had a headache.

He insisted that he would get her luggage, and she was worried for him because those two suitcases were so heavy. In addition to the gifts she got them she brought them homemade baked goods. She walked behind him with her handbag and hand luggage. He showed her the bedroom that would be hers for the next ten days. He explained with pride that he had prepared it especially for her so she would have her own amenities while he used another bedroom.

She was about to take a shower and then head to bed when she decided to get a glass of water from the kitchen. She bumped right into Phena, who was elated to see her and embraced her breathlessly.

"Welcome to our home, Roberta. Get some sleep, and we will talk in the morning."

She woke up that Tuesday, New Year's Day 2002, in his mother's home. She knew it was quite late, and when she looked at the clock it was already after midday. She must have been so knocked out to wake up so late.

I have to call my family back home so they know I arrived safely.

She soon learned that had already been taken care of, but she decided to call them later any way. She was always independent and mindful of others, so she decided she would go purchase a phone card to use during her stay as soon as Aubyn was able to take her.

He had taken few days off from work while she was visiting, but they were split days. So he was off for at least another day then back to work then off again for another two just before she returned home. He worked as a systems engineer for a trucking company where he built and maintained the computer network for the entire company.

She got dressed in a warm, black turtleneck blouse with gold buttons and a knee-high khaki skirt. She felt cute, and he really liked seeing her in her skirts, but with this weather she knew she would definitely have to start wearing pants.

She was accustomed to combing her hair in a ponytail rather than letting it flow. This morning she decided against that and really let it down. It looked nice to her.

As she approached the kitchen she saw Aubyn and his mom busy in the kitchen preparing what must be brunch.

"Hey there," he said. "I just barely got up myself. Sweetie, I did not know what your preference was so I took a chance and did an omelet, turkey ham, and some hot chocolate."

"Thanks, but I could have come out and helped with that. I will get the dishes then."

"So, Roberta, only you could get my son in the kitchen to make a meal. I mean, he helps me with the dishes and is very thorough with pots and pans and cleaning up my stove, but to prepare a meal? No, not him."

Roberta blushed and was unsure how to respond. "Um, well, I guess he likes to surprise us with what he really can stir up in the kitchen then."

As she glanced across the hallway she noticed on this New Year's Day that there was a Christmas tree still decorated and a lone gift sitting under it.

"Go on over there," Aubyn said. "You were the one person missing on Christmas Day."

She had absolutely not been expecting anything. It was a large, square gift wrapped in a delicate gold paper. The words, *Merry Christmas, Sweetie, From Aubyn,* made her heart flutter. It was such a rush of excitement; it was intense.

He walked with her to her room and insisted, "Open it. This is way overdue. We all enjoyed ours. Now you should too."

She pulled at the cords very cautiously and ever so tenderly pulled at the gift paper as if trying to preserve it. "It's OK, Sweetie. Rip it open. It doesn't matter if the paper is torn."

She gasped. "A laptop! My very own computer!" Tears rolled down her cheek as she thought of how long she wanted one, not knowing when she would be able to afford one. She had car payments. She was paying for her apartment, and she had been paying her orthodontist fee monthly for what felt like forever. She thought there was just no way she was getting a computer any time soon.

She grabbed his neck and hugged him. As usual in his soft voice he said, "It's OK, hon. Glad you like it. Didn't think you'd like it that much. Glad you are happy. Now quit the tears."

She smiled. It was a small, neat Toshiba, gray in color. It was really hers. She was still stunned that he did this for her.

They started talking about how they could now send each other emails and chat online. It would not be so bad after all, she thought, because they could now be in touch whenever they felt like it, and that would be very often. The only thing was that she did not have an email address and had never sent an email in her life. It was embarrassing, but with Aubyn she could tell him, and it would be OK. He would not make her feel stupid or anything.

"Let's have you set up with an email account," he said, and then helped her create one at Yahoo!, her very first email address. He showed her how to send and receive emails, and it seemed simple. "Come on, let's test this out."

He walked briskly across to another room and logged into his own computer. He asked, "Did you receive my message?"

She had not, and she wondered if she did something wrong. She feared he might think she was not quick-witted.

"Give it a minute, then hit send and receive to force it."

Yes, her very first email, it was a special moment. *Sweetie, just a test,* it read.

She hit the reply button and wrote, *Got it.*

They returned to the kitchen as her stomach was truly growling. The door chimed, and there was Dean coming through the front door with two large parcels. He apparently had gone to get fresh bread and pastry. He came in with a haughty, "Hey, Roberta. So you made it. Welcome to our humble home."

She knew it definitely was not humble.

He then said, "I am off today, so I have time if you want to see around the neighborhood. That is, if bigger bro here does not have any immediate plans."

"No problem, go show her around. I still have tomorrow off. Is that what you want to do today, Robby?"

So it was agreed after the meal she and Dean would drive around the small city of Raleigh Heights.

There was still one member of the household that they had not met yet, and that was their stepdad Rupert—actually, two members, because there was also Chelsea, Aubyn's dog, which was definitely a member of the family. She did not wait too much longer to meet the other two.

Rupert proved to be a grumpy man. She was a little uncertain when he entered the kitchen. He was not smiling, and he spoke in a stern way and quite loudly too. He turned to his wife to demand, "What are we doing for dinner? I am heading on the road. If you need anything, tell me now before I leave."

Phena answered him loudly. Roberta wondered why they were yelling. "No, I have that planned already, but where are your manners, Rupert? Didn't you see Roberta?"

"I see her, but since nobody said anything to me I figured it was not my business," snarled Rupert.

"That's not true. We have been talking about Aubyn's friend for the past few weeks as her trip approached," retorted Phena.

"Well, pardon my manners, Roberta, but how would I know it was you? It could be anyone else. I am usually the last to hear what goes on in this place," said Rupert with a hint of a smile. She began to let her guard down as he spoke. He did not seem so harsh after all. She soon learned that he yelled and his wife yelled back because he had real problems hearing, especially in the left ear, and was too proud to wear a hearing aid.

The house was huge. She was given a quick tour by Momsy, as she affectionately called Aubyn's mom. Across from the kitchen was a long, wide patio with several windows beautifully dressed by elegant drapes. As she pulled the drapes away the backyard was revealed. It was a big yard with several fruit trees that were mostly naked as the winter was upon them with little mercy.

She stood looking through the window and noticed the dog's kennel. She figured she might not see her as she must be quite snug in there. Just then a tall, pretty, and slightly overweight brown and black dog emerged and stared back at her through the window. She looked like a mixed breed, partly German shepherd and partly something else, with cute but small floppy ears.

This is Chelsea, she thought. She soon realized Aubyn was standing behind her. "I knew those adoring eyes could not be looking at me, so it was you she was looking at," she told him.

"Robby, Chelsea and I go way back. I got her as a pup at this company I was working at four years ago. Someone found her in the parking lot and asked a bunch of us if we wanted her. Everyone said it was a cute little thing, but they already had dogs. When I looked at those eyes I was a sucker for her right away. Guess you could say I have been stuck with her since. You see, I do have a long-standing history with the female species," he joked.

Although that was a joke, Roberta found herself feeling jealous, wondering if he were implying something else and thinking of him with other women.

She heard Momsy's voice, rushing as usual with apparently too much to do. "So let me take you down to my bedroom, but pardon me, I have paperwork all over my bed and my dresser. I wonder when I will ever get done with that."

Roberta discovered she was not joking. Literally half of her bed was covered in paperwork. She wondered if she could make sense of all that and if she were able to find anything in that rubble.

Roberta soon learnt that the pile grew with each day as Phena inherited more paperwork ranging from reports to be written or bills to be paid. Momsy also had a hard time resisting the phone. Time management was a major issue for her and hence the never-ending cycle.

She had a spacious bedroom with a walk-in closet filled with shoes and hats of every color and style. She had several suits hung up and several unopened packages that she said she had not had time to open. Her taste in clothing was that of a highly classy woman.

The next stop was a small room next to Phena's, then Aubyn's music room. His impressive keyboard was on a shelf, and the room was full of speaker boxes and headsets, amplifiers, and a computer connected to it all. It was obviously set up by an avid music lover. The other side of the room boasted a grand piano that needed some fixing. He also had an organ, which she figured was what he used mainly as it had an open music book on it.

When she completed the tour she realized that Phena bought the house originally with four bedrooms and added two more, as well as an informal sitting room across from the formal one.

Dean had been waiting patiently all this time. Roberta grabbed her coat and was about to head out when Aubyn stopped her.

"I think you are forgetting something," he said and kissed her on the cheek.

She saw the front of the yard properly for the first time, and the flowers were gorgeous. Dean told her that the flowers got most of his mother's time and usually were the first things she tended to on a daily basis no matter what else needed her attention.

Raleigh Heights was a small city, but she liked what she saw. They were back in a little under two hours. Dean was the perfect guide, telling her as much as he knew and pointing out some of his favorite food places.

By the time they returned, Momsy was in the kitchen already done preparing salmon, which she was serving with yams and potatoes and salad. Aubyn was looking at his watch and smiling.

"I did not want to eat without you 'cause my mom would let me have it, but everyone around here knows I don't like being hungry," he said.

New Year's Day was coming to a close. It was a great start to a new year, she thought, and so far she was having a good time. It was now after 8 pm, and she was about to learn how entertaining this young man could be. He had a passion for instrumental music and was a good musician. He took her to his music room and was so into his music it seemed he was in another world. When he played, it was soothing and had a romantic note to it. She was enjoying the moment. They did not say much. They just let his fingers do the talking on the keyboard.

She especially liked one he played by the group Foreplay. Later he played "Sweet Love," by Anita Baker, and she had a hard time deciding which was her favorite.

The next day, Wednesday, which was the day after new year's day, she woke up early enough around 9 am. After all, she was on vacation so sleeping in was allowed. Aubyn would return to work on Thursday. He told her last night that he hoped she would like the San Diego Zoo because he wanted to take her there.

The ride was two and half hours long, and she really enjoyed being driven. The scenery was picturesque. She was captivated by the expanse of land and the folds of the mountains. The island where she had been born had lots of elegant green mountains, some of which appeared a delicate blue from a distance, especially the renowned Blue Mountain, which boasted an elevation of over 7,400 feet. She had only visited two other states, Florida and New York, but never noticed such folds or contours in the mountains there.

It felt great being in his company, just the two of them. When they got there Aubyn said, "Let's see how much of a country girl you really are because we are riding in the tractor today. Guess what? We will also be driving closely to the animals, and if I remember correctly, the giraffes like to poke their long necks down at their visitors. Let's say they are just as curious as we are."

He took pictures and video recorded almost every detail. After the tractor ride they walked for a while, as she pointed at cute little monkeys hanging from the branch of a huge tree. There weren't any animals she had not seen on previous trips to the zoo years before, but any outing with Aubyn was fun.

They stopped on the way back home at a Chinese restaurant. The meal was OK, but she was not really hungry as they had packed sandwiches from home and had eaten those earlier.

It was dark when they pulled up in the garage. Roberta undid her seat belt and had her hand on the door when he stopped her. The garage light went out. He reached across and gave her a deep, seemingly unending kiss. She started to respond and forgot for the moment where they were, until a light came on in the garage. Dean was parking right next to them.

She was not sure if he saw the kiss, but she felt so embarrassed. He did not have to see to figure out that some intimacy was occurring. Dean glanced in their direction, smiling, and didn't tarry. He headed indoors. The interruption apparently brought them back to reality, and they decided it was time to head inside as well.

"Goodnight, dear. I hope the evening was not too uneventful for you, but I enjoyed the day with you," Aubyn said. "I will be back at work in the morning so I am going to shower and turn in."

She did the same as it had been a long day, but a good one.

It was not the same when she woke up and he was not there. There was not much to do, and she feared it would be a boring day. She found herself feeling a little depressed. She got up to a quiet house with no one in sight.

Dean would be at work. Rupert probably had gone to see some game, and Phena probably was already up and buzzing. She went to help herself in the kitchen when she heard Phena come in.

"Hey, I have several errands to run on the street. Come out of the house. I will be leaving in another hour."

Over the course of the day, Roberta found herself vowing silently that this would be the last time she went out with Momsy. In the car Phena said she would be stopping at the bank, a discount mall, and the grocery store, but they ended up going to many other places that were not planned. The time they spent at each store was more torture. Roberta now realized that Phena had a difficult time making up her mind, and she was not organized at all.

What should have been a pleasant outing became exhausting. Momsy was very kind, though. In a department store she held up clothes, saying, "Roberta, this would look good on you. Try it." She picked several items for her, and they were all really nice. "You like it?" she asked as she picked out an attractive pair of lavender heels that went well with one of the outfits.

"They are all nice, but I can pay for some of them. I did bring a little shopping money up with me."

"Keep your money today. Today is my treat."

She sensed that she could be a little controlling when Roberta said, "OK. I like all except this one. I think the color is too much for me." It was a bright orange, stylish, but she just did not like it in that color.

"Girl," Momsy said, "you better get real. You don't know style. This would really suit you, and you should take it. If you still don't like it, although I see no reason you shouldn't, I'll bring it back."

Shopping for clothes took time, and this was not the plan. She was grateful, but, oh, what a day it had been. By the time they got home Aubyn was already there wondering where she and his mother were. He did not see anything prepared for dinner, so he popped two DiGiorno pizzas in the oven and figured they should all just do a quick dinner.

"So I see my mom had you all over town today," he said. "I forgot to caution you, but you will soon understand my mom lives in the stores. I bet she left half of the stuff in the van 'because she knows what Rupert would say if he found out. She will gradually bring them in as small bits when Rupert is not noticing. He always says he has never seen a woman with more clothes and shoes and still buying. I guarantee that she will have you out for the rest of the week."

Roberta thought, *Oh, I don't think so.*

But he was right. Like clockwork every day his mom had some errand or other to run and was ever complaining that she could never find time to get things done. The next few days Roberta found herself going someplace or other with Phena. It was OK, but she wanted more for her vacation.

She would be returning home next Wednesday, which meant she had less than one week to go. Aubyn would not be off again until the following Monday, just two days before she was to leave. She still had a few items she wanted to bring back for some family and friends. She wanted to do that when Aubyn could take her because going with his mom meant several other impromptu stops that could take an entire day.

Each day went by in a similar fashion. She got up to see Phena, who got off duty in the mornings then stopped outside to tend to her flowers then came in sighing about all she had to accomplish. Roberta typically assisted with the meals and dishes in order to take some of that work load off Momsy. Phena then complained about the paperwork.

"Momsy," Roberta said. "I wish I could help you with that, but I really would not know where to start. I think you would do well with a secretary." They both laughed.

The days seemed to roll by rather fast. One morning she awoke to a beautiful day. She knew it was special, but, still drowsy, she forgot why she had set the alarm clock. Then she smiled and remembered she would be going to his church for the very first time.

They arrived at the church at 9:30 am. The parking lot had several cars already even though the church was average in size.

They got there before his mother and brother as he claimed he did not want to risk waiting from them and arrive late. "I don't want us to make a 'grand entry' he muttered..

"Robby," he continued, "My family and I have been members here as long as I can remember, but today I have a weird feeling in my gut. I feel like all eyes are on me."

He sighed then they picked a spot, third bench from the back on the right hand side of the church. "They have never seen me with anyone other than my family at church so surely they are having all sorts of thoughts and are bursting to know."

It was time for the welcome. "Br. Aubyn," Pastor Don said. "A blessed day to you, and could you introduce your visitor to the church?" He gestured for her to stand.

Her Visit to His Overseas Home

"Good morning, everyone," Aubyn said. "This is my friend Roberta visiting with us from the Caribbean. Please pray for her safe return home as she departs Wednesday the 9th."

She was not required to say anything, so she just waved and smiled.

The rest of the service went by, and the message was mainly about thanksgiving for the past year and blessings for the new one. At the end of the service the pastor and elders were at the exit greeting as everyone filed out in an orderly manner.

They were warm and welcoming. Aubyn seemed to know everyone, and they all knew him too. A potluck was going on in the church hall, but they did not stay. They saw Phena and Dean heading in that direction, meeting and greeting as they went.

As they walked out he was stopped by every second person who passed by. The church yard had a beautiful lawn, and he, as usual ever prepared with his camera, grabbed Br. Benjamin to "do the honors," as he called it.

It was a dashing picture. He was tall and slim with slightly bowed legs and seemed to lean sideways in the shot. He was dressed in a gray suit and a burgundy tie with a gray shirt, and to top it off his glasses had a nice dark tint that transitioned with the sunlight. She was in a beautiful lime green dress that was knee-high and a long-sleeved jacket of the same length.

It was a lovely day. She felt blessed from the service, and she kept one of the programs as a souvenir. It felt like family at the church. She felt so at home it reminded her of her own church. They drove home slowly, and he deliberately took a different route on side streets to prolong the drive. She felt so close to him, and she wondered what it was going to be like when she had to leave.

The rest of the days went by even faster, than before, it was already Tuesday. She would leave tomorrow. He looked a little sad when he knocked on her bedroom door that morning, not the usual big bright eyes smiling at her. "I wanted us to do something special today, but I leave it to you. Anything you wanted to do?"

They had been utilizing his after work time to get the other things taken care of for her. She had already packed, with just a few things to throw in at the last minute, so that was settled.

She said, "I would like a quiet dinner somewhere simple, not extravagant, where there is some good food."

He smiled. "That's easy, I know just the place. Is 5:00 pm good?"

They settled on that. They did nothing in particular leading up to the time, just talking and hanging out and enjoying being together.

She went to get a shower around three o'clock. She already knew what she would be wearing: a black and white close-fitting cotton dress. The outfit had thin straps, and she knew she could not think of going outside in just that. She grabbed a cute double-breasted white jacket. She knew she looked great. She was 110 pounds and only five feet, three-and-one-half inches tall, and the clothing fit perfectly.

He was not dressed up. He wore a dark pair of pants and a bush jacket-type burgundy shirt. When he knocked to see if she were ready he said, "You look superb. I like the way it fits you, missy. You will have those guys looking at you. I don't mind as long as they look and don't touch." He grinned at his comment.

It was a romantic evening. They went to a Mongolian restaurant, very quiet and different. She had never seen food prepared like that before. All their order was picked up raw and undone and piled high in a dish.

He said, "I'll give you a hint. It all will shrink, so pack it in as much as you can. You'll see."

She did see what he was talking about. She watched as they took her huge dish of shredded chicken and vegetables and placed it on a huge, round hot metal stove with a large flame, and it was done before her eyes in no time. It was good, and they savored it and enjoyed most of the meal in silence as they knew it would be a long time before they would again be together in this fashion.

The drive home was about thirty minutes, and they got home before 7 pm. She had enjoyed a good evening, but there was such a sadness. She did not want him to see her cry so she gave him a short kiss on the mouth and said an early goodnight.

It was Wednesday, January 9th. She did not even remember it was the birthday of one of her friends. It was so bittersweet. The day sped by and before she knew it she was hugging Momsy and Dean and even Rupert, who never had much to say, good-bye.

There was an emptiness. She tried her hardest not to cry, but she felt the tears falling on her face and wiped them away. Aubyn was solemn and quiet on the way to LAX. She did not want to say too much because he might think she was a softy if she tried to talk and choked on the words.

Her flight was 9:50 pm, and she was there by 8:30. After he helped her with her luggage check-in it was time to make her way upstairs to her terminal. He had a stone face on, and she tried to smile. They embraced tightly for an extended period.

"See you later," she said as she kissed him, not wanting to stop and not caring who saw it. She smiled as she whispered, "I love you."

He responded, "Me too."

As she made her way through immigration she saw him standing at the top of the stairs looking in her direction. He seemed so motion-less. As she continued walking away to Terminal D she knew he was still there even though she could no longer see him clearly except for his army green shirt.

CHAPTER 4:
HER RETURN
TO THE CARIBBEAN

S he was in transit for over an hour before boarding time. The sadness and the heaviness were immense; the grief was as though someone had died. They called for boarding, and as she looked through the glass into the darkness she too felt like her light had gone out.

It was going to be a long flight, between five and six hours. She got a window seat in row seven. As she looked through the window she wished she could fall asleep. She just wanted to wake up and be home. There was no fun in flying without a companion after being with her loved one these last few days.

She never slept during a flight. She just could not. She just felt she should be awake. Luckily most of her flights were relatively short, though this was the longest. She sat there lost in thought and was surprised when the pilot announced they were two hours away from Sir Donald Sangster International Airport in Montego Bay.

In her mind's eye Roberta envisioned that Aubyn had gotten back home hours ago. It would be around 2 am, so she pictured him in his bedroom. He often fell asleep in his favorite black robe, and she figured he was nice and snug, while she was only slightly reclined and still awake.

They were reminded to remain seated, and she could feel her ears pop as they descended rapidly. It was approximately 7 am when she landed. It would only be 4 am back in California, so she figured by the time she drove home it would be good time to call.

She did not take long to claim her luggage, and she could see her friend Rhea and her mom waiting to pick her up. They had so many questions for her, all so excited and waiting expectantly for what they thought would be intriguing information. She did not feel like talking much, but smiled at them and made excuses of being tired.

"How was the trip? Did you like it? Do you think you could like it enough to live there?" Rhea asked.

"Don't you think that's looking too far ahead? Who says we will even need to think about that?" Roberta laughed at the question.

"Well, it's only natural you must have some hope of a future relationship or you would not have taken the trip in the first place, right?" said her mom.

She was hoping the conversation would shift to general talk and thanked the Lord when it did. They spoke about nothing in particular, from her mom's work to Rhea's to what she had missed on the news while she was gone.

She was back in Mandeville before she knew it. She arrived home close to 10 am. All she could think of was calling him to let him know she was back home safely, and she longed to hear his voice. She did not want to disturb his sleep, but she called anyway.

He answered drowsily. He was yawning so much, but his gentle, soft voice was still happy to hear her. "Hello, Sweetie. You home already? It feels like you are still here, but I am in the other room and you in this one.

"I was wondering if I should tell you this, but I did not change the pillow cases that you slept on yet. I still smell your scent, and can you believe I found two strands of your long brown hair on my bed and I kept them?"

She wanted to cry. It was so sweet to hear his voice, to hear what he said. In her heart she asked, *Why, Lord, do I have to go through this? Why?*

She was tired. She had not slept in more than twenty-four hours, and she was beat. Her friend Rhea returned to her own home, and her mom decided to spend the night with her.

After talking with Aubyn she pretty much did only the necessary. She got a shower, turned the phone low in her bedroom, and went to lie down. It felt so good to be fully stretched out in bed. She was asleep in no time.

When she got up it was looking dark outside. She had slept for over ten hours, and she still felt groggy. She and her mom had talked for a while as she fixed herself a snack. Her mom was yawning because she had been up since 3:30 that morning to get dressed for the journey to the airport. She was ready for bed by 8.

Roberta still had three days before returning to work on Monday morning. She had been away for only ten days, and she had so many things to get done, so it was catch-up time. Friday she arose early and did her regular errands, back to her regular routine. She went that same Friday to have her Internet set up for the very first time, which was very exciting.

She knew Aubyn would be thrilled to get an email from her, and if she sent it to his pager it would happen immediately. What a surprise he was going to get! She sent two messages, a longer one to his regular email and a shorter version to his pager.

Hi, dear. Guess what? I'm online. Isn't that fantastic?

She checked her email, and in less than five minutes he responded with one line from his pager, *OK, great @ work talk later*. He did not sound excited, and she was disappointed. He was at work, but he could be a little more excited, she thought. But she consoled herself that he would get in touch as soon as he could. She logged off the computer. She had lots to do, so she continued with her tasks.

Her mom had returned to her own home, and Roberta was now back from her errands in a lonely house. She sat down to watch the seven o'clock news, but the phone rang at the same time. She tried not to run for it, but she did with a bubbly, "Hello!."

Clint's voice was ever distinct, deep and low. "Welcome back. I didn't think you were ever coming back. I just decided to try the number, and bingo, jackpot. So when were you planning to let me know you were back?"

She was happy she hadn't said, "Hello, Aubyn," although she had been so sure it was him. She definitely did not want to hurt Clint's feelings, but she promised the next time she saw him she would let him know about her boyfriend.

With a start of surprise, she realized she had referred to Aubyn as her "boyfriend." She never had before, and it felt strange, but she thought she liked it.

"I returned yesterday," she told Clint. "You know how that goes, jet lagged and all. Of course, I would let you know at least in the coming week."

He asked, as usual, "When can I see you?"

"I return to work on Monday so I can't say just when, but we'll see. Next week sometime, maybe."

He talked for a while and then apparently received a beep that might have been a personal call or a page from the hospital. Whatever it was, he was gone, and that was a regular thing that had happened ever since she first met him.

Roberta was listening for the phone because she was not going to call Aubyn. He should call her because she already tried to reach him. Then she remembered her laptop, her very own Toshiba laptop. She still did not remember sometimes that she had it. She still could not believe that he even got it for her. She felt so moved by the expensive gift. She had never ever accepted a gift from a man before.

She logged on right away, and he had left her a message: *It is 6 pm on my end so I know its 9 pm over there. I'm not sure if you have time to say goodnight, but if you do, please respond. I will be checking my email every fifteen minutes to check for a response. We could do a live chat. That would be a nice goodnight for me.*

She responded, *I am still awake. I definitely have a few minutes.*

It seemed like he was there waiting or had just walked into the room because he responded almost instantaneously.

They were online for at least the next hour until she realized she had to get some sleep. They talked about her time there and how it had gone by so fast.

He asked, "Remember that I told you about finding strands of your hair in my room? I am finding them in my car and on my chair by my computer. This may sound weird, but I find myself saving them."

She laughed. She truly liked this guy more and more. She knew him a little better now, so she imagined his big, bright, pretty eyes growing larger as he got excited. She sighed at the thought of the distance between them.

She felt encouraged as he told her that there was a program available for free that would allow them to talk via her computer. "Besides that, there is little delay, so hesitation is not apparent and it is quite clear. Setting that up and walking you through it will be my next project."

It sounded so promising. She really felt happy.

"We could even go a little overboard and add the Webcam later so we could see each other," he said.

She was amazed. She did not think that was even possible to see each other thousands of miles away. It seemed unreal.

January went by rapidly, and Roberta was amazed to realize it was already February. It has always been a special month for her. There was

Valentine's Day on the 14th, the 23rd was her birthday, and the 24th was Aubyn's birthday. Interestingly too, the 25th was his brother Dean's.

February 14 came, and the very first caller was Clint, who invited himself over. She was going to make it known to him no later than that day that she had a friend, and they truly liked each other with many things in common. She knew how he would mock her and laugh when he learned that her friend was overseas. He most likely would ask how she had found him and if she ever thought anything would come of that.

One thing with Clint: he was a very straight-forward person. He did not beat around the bush and was too practical most of the time. He was not rude, but he could come across like that when he got into that mood.

She decided to call Aubyn via their computer program. She could see he was online but was not hitting the accept button when the call was coming in.

She decided to check periodically. She was happy when she saw he was now trying to call her. She saw his code name, "Chatto," appear on screen, and she quickly accepted the call.

Oh, that voice that she did not think she would ever tire of hearing.

"Hi, Sweetie. Hope I am the first person to call you this morning."

She wanted to make him happy and answer in the affirmative, but of course he was not.

She left his question hanging, and he said to her evidently without noticing, "Unfortunately, even though today is my day off, I had a client call, and I was remotely assisting. I had the problem figured out pretty quickly, but all that fine tuning to get it just right took way too much time. So anyway, I am all ears now and will be yours for the next several hours if you'd like." He said this last with a gentle chuckle.

She wondered, as usual reading too much into things, why didn't he say "I am yours for all times if you want me to." She sighed, hoping that would happen someday, but wondering how considering she lived thousands of miles away on the island while he was in California and she did not wish to immigrate. She just did not want to think about that.

The Lord always worked things out, she told herself. This would be no different.

She was half-listening for a knock on the door, but they had been talking online for over an hour and Clint had not turned up. He was good at that. He would call and then turn up much later. She was happy for that this time because she did not want to give Aubyn an excuse for disrupting their alone time.

At last, she did hear a knock on her door, and her heart leapt. *Oh no, she thought. Why did he bother to turn up?*

She told Aubyn she would call him right back as she had a visitor. When she opened the door her half-smile broke into a huge one. Her hand went over her mouth and a gasp. A nicely dressed delivery guy stood there, and she saw a card poking out of a gorgeous bouquet that read, *From Aubyn to my sweetie.*

She was blown away. She thought of his being so many miles away and how he went through all that trouble to order her such beautiful flowers. She was now crying. This was so unexpected and so sweet, she thought.

It was a large bouquet, so beautiful with so many different colors. She was not the best on the names of flowers, but she saw orchids, hibiscus, several stems of red roses and some white ones too, and then there was the beautiful lavender zinnias and peach anthurium from Yvonne's Flowers that she knew so well. He must have ordered it online or gotten some information from her mom at least. It was such a surprise!

She jumped online and dialed him. She felt like she could not care for him anymore than she did at the moment. When he answered she told him how much she loved them and how beautiful they were. Then she asked, "How did you even get away with this and I did not suspect? You made my day ever more special."

"I do like to surprise you, Sweetie," he said.

They spent another two hours online while she periodically got up either for a glass of water or run to the restroom. She could not have asked for a better valentine.

Clint came quite late, and she just wanted to savor the time she had spent with Aubyn. He got there after 7 pm. He did not get her anything, and she was not expecting anything. She did not want anything either. He mainly asked if she had cooked and talked about how hungry he was. She offered him dinner and just proceeded to tell him everything about her new relationship.

He laughed, and, just as she thought, he asked in a matter-of-fact kind of way if she seriously thought seeing him so infrequently could materialize into anything. He stayed around talking for a while not taking anything that she said seriously. His behavior was as if she said nothing—same as usual, nothing changed.

Before she knew it was her birthday. Birthdays were very important to her, and she typically remembered family members' and friends' birthdays. No surprise, Aubyn called her. He had gotten her the Webcam like he promised and had gone over the steps with her. They were straightforward, and he decided there was no better time for the debut of the Webcam to her home.

She set up her laptop on the desk her mother had given her as a birthday gift the previous year. She found a nice spot on the desk and placed her Webcam there.

He asked, "Are you ready to see me? Hope you are 'cause I am surely ready to see you."

She did not know what to expect. She was hoping the technology was as good as he said. She had doubts because she really did not even think that could occur. She only recalled that on one of her favorite childhood cartoons, *The Jetsons*.

She heard him say in his usual soft voice, "Hello, I can see you."

She was not ready yet as she did not realize her camera was pointing at her. She quickly shifted it to her dressing table instead. She wanted to look just right.

Luckily he was such a gentleman. What if she had not been fully dressed? It was amazing to think over the wires thousands of miles away he could see her. She thought she must sound stupid if she kept talking that way because all this was normal technology for him.

When she believed she was ready to be seen by him she refocused the camera on herself. She had put on a cute little sleeveless red dress.

"You look nice, Sweetie," he said.

She saw him too. He was in a light colored shirt. She was not sure of the color, but she could clearly see his face, although as he gestured the movements were delayed.

It was refreshing seeing him and knowing that everything she was seeing was happening right at that moment. "Dear, I would like to see your room just so I can fall asleep with that picture in my mind," he said. "If that's OK with you, that is."

"No, that's OK, no problem at all." She angled the camera as much as she could, but unfortunately the cord was not long enough for him to see beyond her bedroom. He showed her around her room at his house, but she had a vivid memory of that bedroom already. He then tried to show her a few strands of hair that he supposedly saved, but she could not see them.

"OK, I take your word for it. After all these weeks you still find strands of my hair in your bed, on your chair, in your car." She figured he was joking, but he convinced her that it was no joke. She thought it was so sweet of him even to mention it.

Her birthday turned out to be special. In addition he mailed her a small check, which she received a day earlier telling her to get herself something. His birthday was the following day, and she had sent him a beautiful card she hoped he would receive it on time. She hoped she did not go overboard in choosing the card. It read, *Happy birthday to the man I love.* Now thinking about it she was quite fretful. Would she scare him off by choosing such a card?

She arose early the morning of February 24. She did not want to call him too early. She knew he probably would not be online so soon with the three-hour time difference and all. It was Sunday morning on one of her days off.

She was up quite early that morning. She looked at the clock and saw it was only 6:30 am. She usually slept as late as 9 when she was off, especially on a weekend. She figured she would start her routine chores, which were the regular laundry, mopping the floor, and cleaning the bathroom. During all that she could get the dinner started. The time surely sped by and it was now past midday, which would make it after 9 am in California.

She was always excited to call him, but now she felt nervous. She regretted getting that card. There were so many other beautiful cards there that were subtler. She had bought a phone card, so she could call him directly just in case he was not planning to go online that early.

She dialed his number and managed a chirpy, bright, "Happy birthday." She continued, "I wish you blessings in all you do and that all your wishes and dreams will be realized."

"Well, thanks for those encouraging words, my dear, and I believe it even more hearing them from you." he said. He did not mention anything about the card, and she wondered if he had gotten it at all or he decided not to mention it.

He then said, "I am logging on right now. If you are not extremely busy we can talk online 'cause I don't want your card to run out on you. I know those things are expensive."

She went to her laptop right away and logged on.

"I got your card, Missy," he said. "Thank you, I ... um, like it. It's really nice. I wasn't even expecting anything. Thanks, Dearie."

They talked as usual as if neither of them had anything else in the world to do. He then said with a huge yawn, "Ah, got to get up now. I have a couple things that have to get done, but we'll talk later if you're not too busy. Is that OK?"

She was her happy self again. It was OK; he liked the card. She finished dinner early and as was customary she finished everything else in the early afternoon. She was very relaxed, just waiting to see if he would contact her. He did, and that was how the rest of the evening went. She told him she would rather be sharing the meal she prepared with him rather than eating alone. They both promised that someday it would work out somehow.

The weeks and months were truly passing by sometimes she found herself unsure of what day it was or writing the wrong date until she caught herself. She hardly heard from Clint. He had only passed by once since she had told him about Aubyn, and his visit was very brief as he claimed he was very busy that day. He had asked if she wanted to take a ride with her down the hill to St. Elizabeth as he wanted to visit a cousin down there. She declined as she had things she wanted to get done.

The year also sped by. Aubyn and her called each other almost daily, only missing when he was at work for extended hours and he got in too late on her end. They had become so close, and she was comfortable around him. He was not just her hopefully expected husband, he was her friend. She told him everything from a bad day at work to a disagreement with her mom. She felt so safe with his gentle voice, and he never seemed to tire hearing from her. He was supportive and encouraging with good advice.

It was hard to believe, but since her visit in December—she still vividly remembered it had begun on a Monday—over a year had passed. They were now discussing her next trip. She was saving her airfare because she wanted to pay for it herself just like she had done on her first trip.

She booked her ticket for February 16. She would return March 1. It felt like only yesterday she was planning her first trip there. It was amazing how soon she would be back there, and the excitement was thrilling. There was always so much to do before a trip. She had to get little token gifts for Aubyn and his family, and she wanted to make sure she brought certain items for herself to avoid purchasing unnecessary things when she got there. She already had a list of things she planned to bring back for herself as well as for friends back home.

CHAPTER 5:

THE RAPID ENGAGEMENT

I t was February 16, 2003, and she was seated aboard the huge Air Jamaica airbus on the runway awaiting take off. She felt so happy. She was on vacation. She was on her way to see him. She could hardly wait for the six-hour trip to end, even though they were still on the ground.

The flight did not seem so long this time. After they braced for the touchdown, she could not believe how smooth it was. A group of teachers on the flight was cheering as they expressed shear disbelief. She remembered one of them saying that the landing was so smooth that they could have balanced a bottle of wine on their heads without spilling. It was indeed remarkable. She did not fly that frequently, but it was amazing. It felt as if the pilot came straight out of the air and stopped.

There was no jerkiness or any bump that she could recall when the wheels hit the runway. It appeared virtually possible. The applause was soon making its way through the entire plane as everyone joined in.

The flight was somewhat delayed. The expected time of arrival was 10:05 pm, and they arrived at 10:26 pm instead. She was not too concerned for Aubyn because he never went to the airport without looking online to check the flight's status.

Recalling her last experience, she smiled devilishly. *Well, if anything at least he will be the one waiting this time, not me.* She was seated in row eight, so she was close enough to the front to be out in no time.

She was out to claim her two bags in a jiffy. Everything was so easy, she thought this must be a sign that something good was in store. She felt so happy and so light. Her life felt blissful.

Roberta was on her way out, and without a shadow of a doubt she knew it was Aubyn as she saw him with all his white teeth grinning widely at her. He must have been watching her for a long time while she made her way out. This time Uncle Guy was not with him.

He pecked her on the cheek and had both arms outstretched as he squeezed her way too tight. She buried her head in his chest and took a deep breath as she smelled his cologne. He smelled great. She was actually here, both of them holding each other.

He said, "Come on, dear. Let's get going. You must be so beat, and we do have a journey ahead of us."

The ride home was pleasant. She no longer even felt tired. The adrenaline must have been working overtime. She had discovered last time that he was an excellent driver, very much in control and very careful. He calculated every move. She even noticed that on the freeway he never switched lanes when another vehicle was parallel in the next lane over. He explained that the driver could be thinking of coming over just like himself, and he had to avoid that. He justified it by saying he always looked ahead. With a grin he explained that this was his philosophy in life and she would experience that soon enough.

On the long ride home he mostly had one hand holding hers while he skillfully maneuvered with the other. Only occasionally, when he thought it was absolutely necessary to have both hands on the wheel, did he briefly pull away.

In spite of the long ride to his mother's house and being awake for over twenty hours, she was actually enjoying the ride. As much as he liked instrumental and jazz music he did not turn on the radio. They just traveled in silence. It was just great to be back with him.

She must have slept a little bit. She was sure it was not more than a few minutes. It was either she was more tired than she thought or she was just so confident with his driving. She heard him say, "Wake up, Sweetie. We are home."

Hearing those words, "We are home," sounded right, sounded like something to look forward to in hopefully the near future.

It was quiet when they got in the house. His mom most likely left for work, as she typically did the nightshift at the hospital. Dean and Rupert mostly likely were asleep as it was past midnight.

She already knew her bedroom. The last time he graciously allowed her to use his room as he said it was more convenient with its own bathroom and greater space. This time was no exception as he wished her goodnight and went off to another room further up the hallway.

She rested well, and for a moment when she awoke forgot where she was. She smiled, no longer groggy from the long slumber. Just yesterday she was back home, thousands of miles away, and now after all this time she was back in this very room, his room that would be hers for the next twelve days.

Roberta awoke to the sound of water spraying. It sounded more forceful than the sprinklers. She peeked through the window and saw Aubyn's mom, who must have just gotten in, watering her plants with the hose. The bedroom was toward the front of the house so she could see the front yard easily.

Phena had left her van door open, and Roberta could see several bags on the seats and floor. Unsurprised, based on past experience with her, she knew she had already stopped at the stores before getting home. She also remembered that if the shopping bags were not necessary household items she would be leaving them in the van for days.

She would gradually bring them indoors when the way was clear of Rupert's watchful eyes. She could hear Rupert now saying, "That woman has more shoes and clothes than she has a back to put them on or feet to wear them, and she just keep bringing stuff home."

Roberta looked at the clock and saw it was 9:45 am already. No wonder she felt so rested. She jumped up quickly, got some clothes on, and went out to greet Phena. When Phena saw her she dropped the hose, forgetting to turn it off. It sprayed her a bit, and she skipped over to turn it off.

"Girl, I am so sorry I wasn't off last night so I could welcome you here," she said. "Anyhow, I know Binnie took care of all that. You see how my life is. There is always so much to do. I barely got in and haven't even been in the house yet because I have to see to my plants.

"So how was the trip? How is Dims and everyone doing?" Phena asked.

"Everyone is doing well. In fact, I saw her yesterday as she gave me bammies and roasted breadfruit to bring for you guys."

She said with a twinkle in her eye, "Binnie has been happier than I have seen him in a very long time. He seems to be quite busier than usual too. In fact, I have not even been seeing much of him lately."

Roberta realized that Aubyn's car wasn't in the garage. *He must be telepathic*, she thought because just then she saw his car entering the driveway.

"Hey, Mom," he called. "Hey, Sweetie. I had to run out for a bit. So how did you rest, dear?" He jumped out of the car and went over to hug his mom and then her.

She wondered why he had not waited for her so they could have gone together. Phena pointed out some specific bags she wanted to be taken inside, and they helped with those as they went indoors.

Phena was fussing about Roberta and what she wanted to eat for breakfast.

"Just remind me where you keep things, and I will help myself," Roberta said. "You need to get some rest. You went through all night of work and just keep going. How do you even do that?"

"Girl," she said, "you just don't know. I have been doing this for years, and the nightshift is the best shift."

Roberta did not attempt to disagree because she knew she would not win, but all she knew was losing a night's rest and then not resting adequately in the day prior to repeating the cycle the same night could not be good.

By now Aubyn was helping to get breakfast ready as Phena made it clear that usually in this house everyone helped themselves, except at dinner. Roberta was quite a simple person. She didn't eat much, and she was not a meat fan. She only ate chicken or fish. Roberta got Phena to sit with them for breakfast as she never seemed to have time even for that.

"My mom has some friends in Las Vegas, the Brooks, whom she has not seen in years although they speak on the phone every few months," Aubyn said. "We have been thinking that would be a great opportunity to show you the city and see the Brooks at the same time. We would be killing two birds with one stone."

The trip was planned for Thursday of that week. They rented a van as the return trip was over 400 miles, and Momsy did not want to pack that much miles on her van. They were ready to leave by 7 am, and the trip was close to four hours long, so all things being equal they planned to be there around 11 am. Aubyn offered to drive, while Rupert and Dean said they would assist if he needed a break.

Roberta was making her way toward the back of the Dodge van that had a seating capacity of twelve. The fivesome had lots of room. As she was climbing into the back Aubyn motioned for her to sit next to him.

"Come sit next to me, dear. I think I'll be a better tour guide if you're right here in the front."

They stopped several times on the way as someone either needed to use the restroom or stretch their legs. The scenery was nice to look at, and she was amazed by the large expanse of idle land. As they drove there were several acres of empty land that she thought could be put to good use.

Aubyn never failed to have his video camera and his regular camera handy. He reminded Dean to take shots of just about anything he thought looked interesting. They planned on staying overnight at Circus Circus. They pulled in just around 11:10 am, pretty much as expected. They got two rooms at the hotel. The three guys bunked together, while Roberta and Momsy stayed in the other room.

It was a simple but nice room, and after such a long ride it was nice to shower and relax a little. They all were ready to head out within the hour. They stopped at Circus Circus and went to get lunch as everyone was famished. It was buffet style, and they all piled their plates with different goodies. The food was good.

Aubyn, who normally had a healthy appetite, was quite modest when eating out, she noticed. Roberta returned for fruits while Phena, who had piled her plate high in spite of Rupert's sarcastic comments, returned for seconds even though she had not been able to finish all she packed on her plate the first time.

She flashed Rupert a mischievous grin as she said, "Oh, I gotta have some of that pie, not to mention the cheesecake. I won't leave without that."

He was so accustomed to his wife's attitude he just brushed her off with his hand in apparent disgust.

Dean, with his typical stare, shook his head slowly. "Mom, you never cease to amaze me." But he was not amused. He was very serious.

Everyone was apparently satisfied, and Phena complained that she ate too much. They all walked around for a while trying to figure out what to do for entertainment. They watched a couple very skillful acts and laughed at some silly clowns, but decided to pass on the rides. Several hours passed, and Phena called the Brooks to let them know they were on their way. They were there in less than fifteen minutes.

It was like a reunion as Phena went off in her low, fine voice, "Hey, Betty, it's a long time, girl, but you look so well. I haven't seen you in, what? Over four years, and you haven't aged a day! Where is Pablo?"

Betty explained, "He is doing well, but I get so tired these days because Pablo had a fall and hasn't been able to walk since. He's in a wheelchair, and as you can imagine I have been his feet since." She smiled, but Phena noticed that she moved a lot slower than she normally did, and she had bags under her eyes.

After the hugging and the greeting they went in to find Pablo positioned at the table awaiting everyone's arrival for the evening meal. The dining table looked lavish with several different and attractive dishes, and the aroma left everyone dying to dive into the meal.

Although seated, Pablo was obviously a big man and had a very deep voice. He sounded stern as well and could be easily mistaken for a mean man. It was clear that he was deeply religious merely by listening to his speech.

Aubyn had his arm slightly resting on Roberta's shoulder and was about to introduce her when Pablo's curiosity preceded him. "And who would this person be? Is it Aubyn's or Dean's?" he demanded.

She felt a little uncomfortable. He did not sound at all friendly when he referred to her.

"This would be my friend, Roberta, from the island," he said. "My family has not seen you or Sis Brooks in ages, and Robby has never been to Las Vegas. We thought this would be a better time than any. Also you know my family, you and your wife go way back, and I felt impressed to have you meet my friend sooner than later."

He looked over his glasses at her and then at Aubyn. "Glad you all could come, and you too, young lady." It was subtle, but she sensed something that she could not explain. He then said, "Come, everyone, let's wash for the meal because you know Betty's cooking can't wait, and those who don't know will know. Let's bless and partake."

It was good! There was so much food, and that all of it had been prepared by one middle-aged woman who already had her hands full was simply amazing. There was veggie parmesan made from eggplant and macaroni and cheese that was out of this world. She claimed was made from six different types of cheese. There were yams, colored greens, beef, and black beans with a hint of smoke flavor, barbecue and roasted chicken and red beans.

Dessert was the good old dark West Indian fruitcake with a little rum and wine for flavoring. It was a great meal. Phena, who was critical of every meal, could not find anything to complain about except that she was too full. She joked that this bellyful would last her another month.

They all stayed around the dinner table for about another hour after they ate. Then Roberta jumped up and started to clear the table, and Aubyn and Phena joined in. Rupert looked like he was falling asleep in his chair, while Dean was engaged in what seemed like an intense conversation with Pablo.

Betty said, "Leave it. Leave it. I will get it. I am used to it anyway, and it's my pleasure to cook such a meal because, with Pablo and me alone, I never get to go all out this way. Only when the church family drops by, and that's only on special events."

The trip home was close to four hours long, so they decided to be on their way. It was already after 7 pm anyway, so they hugged and kissed and said good-bye and promised the next visit would not be so far in the future.

Rupert was too beat to drive, so Aubyn decided he would. However, Dean said it was only fair that he drive back since Aubyn did his fair share already. The city was beautiful at nights. The lights were gorgeous, and Aubyn captured just about everything on his camera as he positioned himself toward the window. It was a good trip, Roberta thought, but she too felt tired.

The drive home did not seem as long, and they all decided to head to bed as it had been a long day. Aubyn had to get up early in the morning to turn in the van to avoid being charged for another day.

Roberta had to acknowledge the truth that "time flies when you are having fun." It was already Friday morning, February 21. She had already been there for five days.

She did nothing special on Friday. Aubyn went to work, and his mom was returning to work that night. Roberta wanted to help Phena as much as possible, and she knew her plants were the other thing that took up as much of her time as the kitchen. The telephone was a big setback for her too as she never could seem to get off the phone, but of course Roberta could not help with that.

After breakfast was out of the way Roberta started with washing the dishes as well as the pots and pans. She was not accustomed to using a dishwasher, and so she did everything by hand. She noticed that Phena did not use it either.

After she cleaned up she started chopping up vegetables, washing and preparing the meat, and allowing it ample time to marinate before dinner. She saw a bag of carrots in the fridge, and she thought Phena and the rest of them could benefit from a healthy homemade glass of carrot juice. She scrubbed and chopped them into pieces and blended them.

She then poured the juice through a strainer and added nutmeg and vanilla and sweetened it to taste. They all enjoyed the juice, especially Phena, who promised she would purchase another bag the next day in order for Roberta to make another jug later that week.

Roberta was not quite expecting that. It required a lot of time and energy to prepare, but she promised she would as she was happy if she could assist her in any way. She had seen her going for hours with as little as an hour of rest before heading out to work at 10:30 pm for her overnight shift.

The rest of the days were just about the same, and she did not mind at all as she had a great time in Nevada and thanked them for the experience. She routinely did what she could to assist Phena in the kitchen and mopped the floor for her as well just to get her into bed for at least four hours of rest. She was able to get Phena into bed many times by 5 pm, and it took lots of effort to accomplish that. Aubyn said he did not know that was possible because his brother and he had given up trying a long time ago. Rupert had resigned from that task a long time before that.

Aubyn imitated in a gruff voice, "Talking to that woman is like talking to the wall."

It was a Saturday night, February 22, and this was one time she was planning to be in bed early, but it never happened. Aubyn wanted them to spend a little time together. She was already in her nightdress and curled up in bed. He asked her to scoot over as he wanted to lie down as well. He said he was not planning on staying past an hour because he knew she wanted an early night.

They talked about everything and laughed. He started to mention some sensitive issues, and for the first time since they became serious she was having second thoughts about their relationship.

Roberta was an attractive girl and had been complimented many times on her appearance and choice of clothing. She was very conservative and modest in her dress. She chose to wear only lip gloss to keep her lips moist and a foundation powder on her face to keep her face evenly toned. That was the extent of her makeup.

Her clothes were well-tailored and well-fitted to accentuate her petite figure, and she wore high heeled shoes on certain occasions and chose to go flat on others. She never tried to turn heads because she did not care about that, but she had gotten a number of admiring stares from men nonetheless.

"Robby, why don't you wear lipstick?" he asked. "I know red would look great on you. You could also try a little eyeliner and shape your eyebrows as well. I am used to seeing my mom wear them all my life, and most of the women here wear them. You would look so much nicer."

Her heart sank. After all this time he did not think she was pretty enough. He had been pretending all this time. She wanted to scream at him, but she was speechless. She looked at him in absolute disappointment.

"This is me," she said. "This is how I feel comfortable. I have never had a guy say this to me before."

"I mean, I am not looking for a girl who is too attractive because I don't want to be self-conscious walking down the street while she is drawing too much attention. I just think you would look better with a little makeup."

"Are you trying to say I am not attractive enough for you? Are you trying to say you have your standards, and I have not measured up? To tell you the truth I don't need to be put down by you or anyone. We could forget everything, and I could head home like this never happened. Frankly speaking, I am not sure if I am even interested anymore."

"Roberta, I do not always express myself very well, and I am going to attempt to explain again. I mean, I will grow to accept you if this is how you choose to be, and I have grown to love you even though at first it was hard to accept that you don't dress the way I prefer."

She had held her cool long enough and she could not hold it anymore. "You don't need to grow to love or accept me!" she shouted. "Neither do you need to lower your standards or compromise or any such thing. There are several ideal women out there. Go get one and just leave me alone. Just leave me, and I am sorry I ever saw you ever!"

By now he was visibly shaking, and his voice was trembling. "See, I have been told all my life that I never say things the way I intend them. They never seem to come out right. I am sorry if it came out wrong, and just forgive me. I promise I will work on all that, and as God is my witness, had I known it would come to this I would have kept silent."

She did not answer one word for an extremely long time. With tears in her eyes she said, "We will see. We will just have to see because I just want to go home right now." She was terribly hurt.

He placed his arm around her shoulders and rested his face on her head, and as he stood to leave the room he said, "I will have to pray about this one because I know I will not be sleeping tonight."

She looked at him and said in a very quiet tone, "Don't worry about it. Get some sleep. God will work it out." She did feel sorry for him. She saw tears roll down his face for the first time.

Sunday, February 23, arrived, and she was not sure how it would turn out after their episode last night. It should be a special day because it was her birthday and she would be spending it with him. Then it should be a double celebration as his birthday was the very next day, but she did not know how it would all unfold.

As soon as she got up she noticed he was already dressed as if to go somewhere and was putting an omelet that he did so well on her plate.

"Happy birthday, Sweetie," he said. "I'm glad you're up early 'cause I have a little surprise for you." He sounded very nervous and looked very unsure. He did not look in her face. "Go get dressed, and we will be on our way shortly." He tried hard to sound normal. She obeyed, but the happiness was not there anymore.

They drove, but she was not familiar with the place. She was sure this was her first time coming this way. She began to see huge homes, and she could see the ocean in the distance. The scenery was beautiful. They drove perhaps close to two hours then he stopped to ask a passerby directions to a place she did not quite catch. He did make mention of a pier.

They were not far from their destination because in just about ten minutes they pulled up to a platform. He paid, the platform was lowered, and he drove the car on. It turned out to be a massive boat because they were soon traveling privately in their own car riding on the ocean. The ride was perhaps twenty minutes. It was hard to tell because she wasn't mindful of time. It was a romantic setting, and her emotions were chaotic. She could not be more confused.

They stepped out of the car unto an island, and they went to one of the many shops. They ordered a simple roast chicken sandwich with lettuce and tomatoes and orange juice. He picked a table that seated two and faced the ocean under a huge umbrella. The day was almost perfect considering the storm that had brewed the previous night.

He looked at his watch and said, "We should be heading back by now. My mom will be wondering why we stayed away so long." She wondered why his mom should be wondering. He was an adult, and he did mention to her that they would be heading out on a two-hour trip. She was sure Phena knew exactly where they were.

The ride back was mostly quiet, and she was gradually feeling like herself again. She was still disappointed with his comments last night, but rationalized it away by thinking he was not good at expressing himself. He did say that to her anyway, and he obviously was heartbroken at the thought that she would just call it quits.

She saw that he unconsciously attempted to reach for her hand as he normally did while driving and then withdrew. Again he tried when they were closer to Raleigh Heights. This time he did grasp her hand, and she did not resist. She heard him sigh involuntarily. It sounded like a huge relief.

As they pulled up, she asked in utter disbelief, "Why are there so many cars in your mom's yard?" It seemed like his mom had a party going on, and she just did not feel much like socializing today.

"Hmm, not sure. Let's go see. I recognize my Aunt Nina's, Aunt Pet's, Uncle Guy's, Uncle Gaston's, and my cousins' cars. There is Petrona's, Petrina's, Karen's, and Kerene's car. Maybe they are just throwing my mom a surprise party. After all, my mom has been a stalwart in the family next to Aunt Virginia."

As they opened the door Roberta soon realized the intent of the party. The house had been transformed from how they had left it earlier that morning. There were balloons and a table dressed up in a beautiful lace with a soft lavender and lime green trimming. Everyone yelled out "Surprise!"

Aubyn did not look surprised. He held her tight and said in a whisper, "Dear, please, have a seat." Everyone else was standing, and all eyes were now on her.

There was a beautiful cake in the center with a picture of her in her red, close-fitting, three-quarter-sleeve blouse and her hair hanging long and beautiful. The words on the cake read, *Please, say yes*. She knew now for sure what it was all about. He was on one knee next to her seat with a tiny box in his hand. As he opened the box an expensive-looking piece of jewelry was revealed. It was a pretty gold ring with a huge diamond stone in the center, and the rest of the gold was dotted with perhaps a dozen more tiny diamonds on each side.

No one would ever imagine the intense emotions that rushed through them both as only they knew this special moment had almost been lost just hours before. Roberta's mind took a walk, and she was only brought back to reality when he gently nudged her and asked her the question, "Will you marry me?"

She heard the audience whisper-read what the cake said. She quietly and tearfully said, "Yes," and they sealed it with a prolonged kiss.

There was a quiet jazz music in the background, his kind of music, and she liked it too. Everyone wanted them to cut the cake together, but the picture on the cake was captured so perfectly she did not want to. They both cut it with his hand resting on hers, and there was a loud cheer.

Momsy said, "Come and get a plate. You guys stayed far too long, and Aubyn should know his cousins. They will not get their hands dirty to cook, but they will eat. No one would wait until you guys came because you stayed so long. You would not know, but Aubyn knew so I blame him. Guy prepared the fish especially for you since he knows you only eat fish and chicken, and he thought the escoveitched fish would be a welcome change. The best of it is gone as they all got to it. I am so mad!"

Roberta tried to console her. "It's OK. There is still plenty of food, and I still see some fish left, and besides, I love baked chicken, and it does look good."

Phena was still fuming, but Roberta guessed she was content that she found a plate with a bit of all the goodies that she would enjoy.

It turned out to be a special day. She only wished Dims, Angela, and Gilford could be there. Her brothers Everett and Andrew would undoubtedly have enjoyed the moment too.

When the last car left it was night. There was so much cleaning up to do in the kitchen. Although disposable cups and plates had been used, there were the salad bowls, the juice jugs, and pots and pans to wash and put away. Aubyn headed in that direction to start the task as Roberta joined in and told Phena they would take care of it so she could just go get ready for bed.

After they were done with the kitchen, they were just thinking and laughing to themselves at how ironic it was that the evening in their honor still had them being the ones cleaning.

He said, "Robby, you made me so happy today. You just don't know. Words don't come out the way I intend them to, but I will learn, and I want you to help me."

She knew that came from the heart. His contrition was genuine, and that made a world of difference.

He did not tarry much longer as tomorrow was another early day at work for him. She was glad he was going to work because she wanted to go pick up something for his birthday. She knew exactly what she would get him. It was within her budget as she had gotten US$300 at her bank just for her trip. She had things she wanted to purchase for herself as well as for family and friends, but his gift would definitely be a part of the budget.

Getting to the store was no problem because if Phena didn't have plans she was always too glad for an excuse to go shopping. They went directly to the store where she had seen the items she wanted the previous week.

She got him a pair of nice, brown, soft wear shoes and a matching brown leather wallet. She loved them, and she knew they would look so good on him. She could hardly wait to gift wrap them.

Phena, of course, had them make many more stops on the way back, so when they got home Aubyn was already there. She was content, however, as she had gotten him exactly what she wanted, and the items were at a good price.

He was not expecting anything and opened his packages with pleasure.

"How did you know I wanted a new wallet?" he asked. "I have been wanting to change these and just never got to it." He immediately reached in his pants pocket and retrieved an old khaki green wallet. "I truly needed these." He emptied the old one and started packing his new wallet. "Thanks, dear. I appreciate it and the shoes. I like them a lot too."

So much had happened since she arrived last Sunday. There was almost a breakup and now an engagement. Her mom would be elated as she really liked what she had heard of Aubyn. Her dad, she knew, would be skeptical. She decided she would call him in the morning. He lived in Florida, so she should have enough on her phone card to call. She knew Phena and Aubyn would allow her to call him from their line, but she did not have to so she wouldn't.

The days went by quickly, as was expected. Their conversation lately took on a different tone. They were looking ahead and discussing what it would be like when she eventually came up for good. Phena was beaming all over and jumped the gun too far for comfort when she said, "I have been wishing that before I pass I would like to have a beautiful granddaughter. I dream of putting ribbons in her hair and buying her the cutest little dresses."

Roberta smiled, but did not know how to respond to that.

It was Friday, February 28, 2003, and she was at the airport saying good-bye to the man who within a few months would become her husband. She came up without a ring, and now she was returning home with a beautiful ring on her left hand. It was already five days since he had first put it on her, and it still felt so strange on her finger, but she loved it.

She was normally self-conscious about displaying any form of intimacy in public, but this time she was unreserved. She kissed him deeply on the mouth and for a longer time than usual. She saw his eyes grew larger and brighter as he looked at her during the kiss when it must have appeared too lengthy.

He smiled as he waved good-bye to her and told her, "See you soon. I'm not worried now because I know you're mine and it's just a matter of time."

She said good-bye, but she could not look back because this time she knew she would cry, and she wanted to avoid that.

She was soon on her flight, and her thoughts were all about her mom's expression when she saw the ring. She thought about her friends Rhea and Maxine, who were still unaware, and how astonished they would be. Work was another story, and people at church too, but they would soon get used to it and would quit bugging her after a while. There was just so much planning and things to get done she did not have time to worry about people and their curiosity.

CHAPTER 6:
HIS FIRST TRIP BACK AFTER THE MEETING

I t was Sunday morning, June 29, 2003, and Roberta, her mom, and her faithful friend Sammy were all waiting to see Aubyn emerge from the airport in Montego Bay. Sammy had driven them as Roberta did not want to do two hours of driving at 5 am.

They were all waiting anxiously to see him step outside, except for Sammy who was notorious for wandering around without telling anyone. Dims saw him first and said, "See him there? My son has arrived, the one in the white bush jacket."

There were so many people coming through. Roberta saw someone in the distance in a white shirt, but she still was not sure.

"You mean you don't recognize your man, your soon-to-be husband in just a week?"

It was not until minutes later when the crowd cleared that Roberta could see him fully. She just couldn't imagine how her mom could tell it was he so far in the distance among so many other people. However, her mom was farsighted and she was near sighted, so that would be the explanation.

Dims did not wait for Roberta to get to him first. She made her way from behind the metal rails where all had to wait and grabbed him in a bear hug to squeeze him tightly.

He barely got a chance to put his hand luggage down and to let go of the cart that had his larger luggage and a suit bag.

He looked a little stunned as Dims was not a huge woman, but was quite stout. He was ever the good sport, and he seemed to enjoy the extravagant welcome. He laughed and said, "So good to see you too, Mom."

Roberta felt shy and self-conscious. He turned to her and said, "Come here. Are you having second thoughts about this, Missy?"

"Of course not." She smiled and hugged him. He bent over to kiss her and she turned her cheek because she was sure the penetrating eyes of Dims would not fail to see.

It might have been anxiety and reality hitting Roberta because she was quiet and was not responding to him quite like she used to. She did not think she was experiencing doubts, but her thoughts were flooded with so much, and she did wonder if this were happening way too fast.

"Hey, we got Aubyn. Now where is Sammy?" Dims asked, and then told them to wait there while she scoped the area trying to find him. Surely he had been gone over half an hour.

In no time Dims was back with Sammy walking in his typical rough-neck walk that no one could help laughing at no matter how upset with him. Aubyn was visibly taken aback by this character.

She heard him exclaim, "Watch ya! What kinda walk is this? What is he trying?"

Her answer to him was, "That's Sammy. You will soon know who he is."

He walked over to Aubyn. "Welcome a yard, man. Pleased to meet you. I am sorry 'bout the wait, but had to stretch my legs and meet few friends."

Aubyn looked puzzled, but he figured Sammy was from the area and had seen some of his buddies.

Dims quickly filled in, "You know where I found him, in the midst of two girls taking photos of them and obviously having too much of a good time."

Sammy defended himself. "They asked for my help. What was I supposed to do? I had to be a gentleman and render my assistance."

They put Aubyn's luggage in the trunk of her car and were soon on their way with Sammy and Dims in front and Roberta and Aubyn in the back. He was captivated by the beautiful scenery as they drove through the hills of the parish of St. James.

The trees were so green and lush and in clusters as if constantly nourished by a spring or river. There was also the dark blue ocean behind as they headed north.

He kept saying it felt like a vacation for him, and he could not get over how narrow the streets were and that there were quite a number of huge potholes.

Dims exclaimed that there was a series of heavy rains. She described them as torrential showers that ravaged the roads even while road work was constantly going on. They drove for another hour and reached the parish of St. Elizabeth. The vehicle slowed down as they passed through the town of Middle Quarters, and the vendors rushed to the car with their bags of nicely packed shrimp.

It smelled and looked so good, though only Sammy could not pass without having some shrimp. The stop was much longer than usual as he had to look into at least a few of the baskets and exchange a few comments with the ladies before purchasing three large bags. As usual no one could be upset with him for too long, and he knew it.

In just a few minutes they were passing one of the famous beauty spots on the island, Holland Bamboo. The trees were several feet tall and stretched for about a mile along each side of the roadway.

He said he thought he remembered vaguely noticing this before as they continued driving on, admiring how the road was lined by these magnificent trees. The trees grew toward each other, and as they met at the top several feet high they formed a natural arch.

Dims had a history lesson for them about the historic bamboo trees. She told them that ever since the days of slavery there had been several attempts to chop the tops off, but then they would mysteriously grow exactly as they were. She added "it's an old folk's tale that had been circulating ever since "my eyes were at my knees," What she really meant was the mystery of the bamboo trees has been told since she was a small child.

They had at least an hour to get to Mandeville in the parish of Manchester. Dims traveled up with them since she planned to stay with them for the first couple days to help as the big day was soon approaching.

They arrived there in good time, just over two hours since leaving the airport, and after such a long ride everyone was just relieved to get out and stretch their limbs. Aubyn was right behind her as they went up the stairs to the apartment. As she opened the door he asked, "Where should I place my things?"

She showed him the front bedroom room, which would be his room for now while she and her mom shared the master bedroom toward the back.

It was just great to watch him move around as he made himself at home in her place. She liked that he was not a fussy person and made himself comfortable.

He unpacked only what he needed immediately and then went for a shower. As soon as he ate he said he would call home briefly and just take a short nap. As it turned out, he didn't wake up until morning. She let him sleep as she could tell he was exhausted. One other thing she learned about him was that he snored and, being a light sleeper, she wondered how she would adjust.

Roberta and Dims got up earlier than Aubyn and fixed the national dish for breakfast. They prepared ackees and codfish with roasted breadfruit that was sliced thin and fried. Roberta recalled that Aubyn was terribly scared of eating fish and made sure it was properly deboned.

It was not his own experience that made him scared, but his brother Dean's. As a child Dean had a mishap with a fishbone, and as Aubyn recapped what it was like to watch his brother go through it he said it felt like he too experienced it.

Dims had run into the town early to get him some nase berries and an assortment of mangoes that he would like: Julie, green skin, Hayden, and East Indian. Once he arose, he ate and told them he did enjoy the meal. It was all local produce.

He reiterated, "This is such a vacation for me. I feel I am being spoiled. You guys didn't have to do all this."

As they ate breakfast Roberta asked, "Did you remember that yesterday, June 29th, when you arrived was the original date we had in mind for the wedding?"

"Yes, that's true. I actually forgot that day would have been our wedding." He added with a mischievous grin, "Then there would be no need for me to be in the front room and you all the way down there in that room."

Indeed, the wedding would have been Sunday, but Aunt Lorraine made an uproar about it. As Dims recalled her sister's behavior she got quite upset. Aunt Lorraine's son Kirk-Lance was graduating from high school that very day. She had no qualms about saying that if the date were not changed she would not be a part of it as she had to be at the graduation. She assumed they should make adjustments to accommodate her.

Roberta was very busy at work, and the venue of the wedding was in Portmore, where Aunt Lorraine lived. She had told Roberta, "I think it would be just ideal to have it here since both of you guys saw each other the very first time in my church up here."

It sounded like a perfect idea, except it was two hours from where Roberta lived, and most of her friends and other family members would also have a long trek.

They ended up going along with her aunt's suggestions. The venue she and her mom had in mind was the West Indies College Church located two miles south of Mandeville. Mandeville was just over 2,000 feet above sea level, while the campus overlooked the town.

West Indies College sat on approximately 200 acres of immaculately kept grounds with elegant landscaping. It was not only a picturesque view, but a refreshingly cool climate.

Roberta trusted her aunt to make arrangements for the wedding reception since she lived in the same town where it would be held. It was not only a far journey for her, but she was also busy at work and not due for vacation. Aunt Lorraine made the arrangements for the venue, including the catering service as well as the limousine service, while Roberta sent the money for the expenses.

Her aunt, being such an integral part of the arrangement, thought it was only right that the date be changed from June 29 to July 6 to accommodate her. It was a difficult decision, since for as long as Roberta could recall she had wanted a June wedding. Her mom used to say that June was the month for weddings and she had kept that in her mind. Aubyn too had locked onto the idea.

It ended up causing an unpleasant atmosphere as Aunt Lorraine continued to argue that it was the least that could be done for her. It started to feel like such bad luck. They decided to change the date as they wanted to make everyone happy. She remembered Aubyn telling her, "Yes, go ahead. Let's push it a week later, no big deal. Guess that's what it's going to be like as we meet our extended family."

She hoped he was wrong.

There was no time to waste. There was still much to be done, and her mom was returning to her own home in the morning. Her dad and stepmom had flown in from Florida and had been on the island for three days already, and she had to go see them. In addition they brought several heart-shaped picture frames for the wedding. A picture of Aubyn and Roberta would be inserted into each to be made available as souvenirs for the guests. The souvenirs were made of porcelain and were intricately decorated with ribbons of lavender and lime green, the color scheme of the wedding.

She headed down the hill to Goshen where they were staying at her dad's house. She always liked going there. It was the house in which she had lived until she was five years old when her persons got divorced. It was a lovely home seated on a hill overlooking the small district of Goshen, with four bedrooms and three bathrooms, a total of thirteen rooms. Unfortunately, she had to leave the huge home she and her brother knew to be theirs. It had been very sad.

She shook all that away as she smiled and thought, *Aubyn and I will be starting our own lives soon, and we will do it differently*. She thought they would be good for each other as he too had experienced the trauma of his parents' divorcing.

She went to see Angela and her dad by herself. They were all expecting to meet the groom-to-be considering they have not met him. Her dad did not want the wedding day to be the first time they met. Aubyn, however, was unable to take the trip to see them that day as he was working on a number of things on his laptop. Roberta already knew that her stepmother and dad would be visiting Aunt Marie, who lived in Mandeville only a few miles from Roberta. She therefore suggested to Aubyn that he could meet them at that time.

She thanked her stepmother for choosing such fitting picture frames. They were really beautiful and Roberta was truly appreciative. She had little time and much to do, so she told them she would see them at Aunt Marie's in two days.

She returned home. It was already late afternoon. It was such an interesting feeling she was experiencing. She did not know how to explain it exactly. It was just different. She was driving to her apartment in Mandeville and he was there. Dims had returned to her own home, and it was just the two of them.

Is this how it's going to be? she asked herself. *I really like how this feels.*

As she opened the door to her apartment she smiled widely. So unexpectedly he was there to greet her. He kissed her straight on the mouth in her doorway.

"Hi, Sweetie. I was wondering when you'd be back considering you haven't seen them for a while, but that was quick."

She was not accustomed to displaying affection publically, and she only hoped the neighbors did not observe the kiss. He led her inside to the dining room where he already had food served for them both just ready to be microwaved. Although this was food she and her mom had prepared, it was a nice gesture for him to serve it. He could have just left it until she got there.

They spent the rest of the evening inserting pictures into the little frames. It took quite some time to get them all done. They said goodnight to each other shortly as they went into separate rooms. In only six days things would change significantly, and they would be sharing the same bedroom.

It was already Wednesday morning. They did not get up early, but after they eventually arose they made brunch together before journeying to Aunt Marie's, which was about twenty minutes from her place.

They arrived at her house around one o'clock. They got to the great house and parked around the back across from one of two casitas that used to be maid's quarters. She recognized her dad's car. She had not thought he would be there so soon. He must really be eager to see his sister or very anxious to see his future son-in-law.

Aubyn had never been in a great house and was quite impressed with this one. He was astonished to hear that it dated back to the 1800s and was actually owned by Aunt Marie and her husband. The house stood proudly, a sprawling mansion on six acres of land.

As they drove around she saw two gardeners attending the plants and another man apparently cleaning one of the large tanks. They soon learned that turtles and fish lived in them.

The front of the house was all cut stone work with double arches at the front. There were numerous fruit trees and evergreens. They could see the windmills spinning at moderate speed, and she recalled that Aunt Marie was not totally dependent on the local power company for electricity. They received up to thirty percent of their energy from the windmills and solar panels. They seemed to do a lot better with the windmills than the panels as it was generally without much sunshine most of the time.

The grounds were well kept, and her aunt had told her before that several couples requested having their wedding receptions there. She rarely allowed it, however, as this was her private home for family and friends. She did allow a recommended few for a quick tour at no charge because she said she thought it selfish to keep it entirely to herself. It was without mistake a significant piece of history, and she knew she was lucky to have acquired it.

As they came out of the car, the stained glass window caught Aubyn's sharp eyes. They walked up to the garage door and were greeted by Uncle Wills and Aunt Marie, who stood with excitement right behind him.

"Welcome to our home, Aubyn, and you, Ms. Roberta that we haven't seen for ages," Wills said. "Come on in."

The house still had the original staircase, they were told. It was not a two-story house, but there were some rooms in the basement used as a gym and rec-room. The floor was all wood with a pretty natural color, some of which was original to the house. The owners had done much work to restore it to its former glory and spared as much of the original infrastructure as they could.

There was a picture hanging in the formal living room of the house in its original state, and Roberta thought it was a beauty. Her aunt shared with them that part of the agreement when they made the purchase was that they had to preserve the history. They complied with the strict guidelines when considering any major work on the building and submitted plans for approval before renovations.

Aunt Marie stopped to get juice for everyone while Uncle Wills led them to the front porch where she found her dad and stepmom awaiting them.

"It's about time you two got here," Gilford said. "I travelled twice the journey and got here before you two kids." Roberta knew he was joking in his grumpiness. "So finally, young man, you decided to show up. I thought I would not meet you until I was giving away my daughter on Sunday."

Roberta was glad when her father smiled as only then she thought Aubyn began to relax. They talked about things in general, and the conversation remained light and pleasant. They talked about anything ranging from the weather to the economy. She could see both men seemed to like each other. She also noticed that he was totally at ease with everyone, including Uncle Wills, but she detected some uneasiness about him when Aunt Marie spoke. She was not quite sure what that meant, but she felt a little concerned and figured he would tell her later.

After a while it seemed that everyone was moving around the house and property, though her dad and Aubyn remained on the porch. She was not worried at all because she could tell that they hit it off both from facial expression and body language, and she believed she knew both of them enough to trust her instincts.

After what seemed like over an hour she went over to them and caught the last part of the conversation. She heard Aubyn say, "Yes, I understand for sure what it must mean to be jobless."

She winked at him because she did not want him to disclose too much.

He had been laid off from his job of over five years for the past six months. He has always been a hard worker and very conscientious, but ever since the devastation in 2001 his company had not recovered. He had gotten calls periodically, but they were not consistent, and he was arduously looking for fulltime employment once again.

He had never experienced that before, and it was difficult for him to accept. She knew he was a cautious spender, and she kept encouraging him that he would soon be doing great again. She felt her family did not need to know that he was currently unemployed just before the wedding.

It was already past four o'clock, and she was glad they had gotten through the initial chit-chat without trouble. There was trepidation on her part initially, and she knew he felt that way also, but the meeting went well overall. On the way home they recounted the afternoon with her family. She hoped he would raise any concerns he had at that time, and he did.

"Roberta, I like your family and especially your dad. He is a cool guy, way nicer than I expected."

"I could see that. I got the feeling you were comfortable with my family and that made me extremely pleased."

"Yes but … your Aunt Marie, I hope I'm not misjudging her, but she was not warm toward me like the others"

"Oh, don't worry about her. Believe me, she is just being herself. She is like that with everyone. You'll see when you get to know her."

"I wondered maybe because she has some wealth and perceives me to be someone with little possession"

"Dear, I think you are reading into something that's not there. Believe me, you will soon agree with me."

Tomorrow was already Thursday, and they would be on their way to Portmore by Friday for rehearsal. She would be picking up her dress that same Friday, and she had to sneak it into the house without his seeing it. Her mother always said that if the guy saw the dress before the wedding day it could be bad luck, and that they did not need.

Friday came, and just as she had been lured over to Rhea's house unsuspectingly for a surprise shower weeks earlier by Rhea and Donovan, Rhea got Aubyn out of the house. She took him out for a ride in the town for some infamous Devon House ice cream while Roberta got a chance to whisk the gown into her apartment.

The anxiety started all over again as she realized she had just two more days and the day would be here. This day would change their lives forever. In addition she never had a chance to see the intricate details. So much was entrusted to her aunt: the venue, the catering, transportation, musicians, organists, decorators, and other services as they all related to the wedding. Knowing her aunt was more than capable, she just dispelled any negative thoughts. As the wedding approached Roberta dreaded the separation that would ensue. They had already agreed that he would not commence the filing process as she wanted to get into and complete her program at school before she joined him. They planned that he would start the process after she got accepted into the bachelor's program and six months before the completion date. According to him, this was roughly the time it would take for him to complete the filing process and receive the approval. So many thoughts were whirling in her mind, but as their special day approached she was not going to allow anything to cloud their moment.

She called Aubyn, and they held hands and each offered a prayer, and it felt OK again. He wanted to do the driving to allow her to relax, but she thought she would instead. Vehicles drove on the left side of the road in the Caribbean, while he was accustomed to driving on the right side. He was a quick learner so she knew soon he would be able to, but just not right now. They then loaded up her small car, Roberta went behind the wheel, and they started the journey.

CHAPTER 7:
THE WEDDING

When Aubyn and Roberta arrived in the town of Portmore, it was close to midday. They decided to stop by the church first to pay Pastor Lewis a visit. It was mainly a courtesy call as the church had already been reserved by Aunt Lorraine six months prior, and Roberta had reconfirmed just a month ago.

The church was quite a magnificent edifice. It was one of the highlights in the town. It served the community well and had to be booked well in advance to ensure availability.

Pastor Lewis and Aubyn were meeting for the first time and greeted each other with a handshake and a polite bow. "I'm sure you are extremely excited about your big day. When was it again? Next Sunday or the following Sunday?" asked Pastor Lewis.

Roberta was unperturbed, but Aubyn looked at her in concern. She knew he was a busy man and wasn't expected to recall dates without checking. He documented everything in his diary anyway.

"No, it's actually this Sunday," said Roberta.

The pastor looked a bit uneasy. "Let me check my diary right now."

They both walked with him to his vestry as he went through his diary. He checked, and he did have a wedding for July 6 at 1 pm, but not theirs. Their own was supposed to be on the same date at 2 pm. When they reserved she remembered her aunt telling her that the day was all clear. Now there was no way he would be able to finish that wedding in an hour for theirs to be on time. There was just no way.

She was so startled when she heard Aubyn, who had been quiet up until now. He spoke in a way that she had never heard from him before.

"You need to fix this," he said in anger. "I came to get married, and you are causing my honey and I unnecessary stress that we truly don't need. You need to fix this. You need to fix this right away!"

She had never seen this side of him. He was so angry he was shaking.

Pastor Lewis answered in a stern, but quiet voice. "Do not raise your voice at me, young man. I will not tolerate that." He then turned to Roberta and said, "I will take care of this. Don't worry about it. It's my problem, so let me do the worrying."

They left, and she could not even believe they just had such an exchange. Everything had been so carefully planned. How could this happen? How? She just hoped it would be resolved although she couldn't see how. She had to trust him, and she whispered a prayer.

The saying that misery likes company proved to have some truth to it as another drama was about to unfold. They left just wishing that episode had never occurred, and they were about to learn of another problem.

Momsy and about a dozen others mostly from her church flew down for the wedding on Friday evening. Aubyn had told her that months leading up to the wedding day that his mother had made announcements promoting a Jamaican holiday and mention of the wedding. She recalled him saying, "You know my mom, how she is. She was up there on the church platform twice. She asked, 'Aren't you just longing for a Jamaican holiday? When was the last time you treated yourself? It will be a vacation of a lifetime and a chance to be a part of a milestone in my son's life.'"

Roberta wondered how he dealt with that because he was a very private and reserved person and avoided so much attention.

They stopped at Aunt Lorraine's where Roberta dropped off her things in preparation for being there until Sunday evening. They ate and showered and were trying to relax on the front porch with Aunt Lorraine and Uncle Lou when they were interrupted by the telephone. Aunt Lorraine went to get it. It was Momsy, and she was crying uncontrollably.

They heard Aunt Lorraine say, "Phena, take it easy. You'll make yourself sick. Calm down and tell me what has upset you so. OK, I understand, but that hotel is not bad. There are better ones, even five stars, but you might not be able to get your friends there tonight. We can take care of that in the morning."

Aunt Lorraine brought the phone to Aubyn. "Your mom is quite upset. See if you can calm her better than I can."

He was only on the phone for a short while. Roberta did not know the full gist of the event and was very curious to find out what was going on.

"My mom does not like the hotel that my dad chose," he explained. "You know my dad he lives in the area and is not picky. Knowing my dad, he is looking at convenience and cost so he chose the hotel down the street rather than directing them to Kingston. Kingston is almost thirty minutes away, and they would find five stars there with no problem. My mom is bawling that he led her and her friends to a junkyard rather than a hotel, and she is so embarrassed she does not how to face them when they return home."

He was apparently content that she would be all right because he was quite composed and calm when he rejoined them. It was getting late, and Uncle Lou thought that prayer was definitely needed. He offered a lengthy prayer for everyone, especially the bride and groom. As they both told each other goodnight they hugged and reassured each other that it was going to be alright.

Saturday night was the rehearsal, and thankfully it went well. She had an excellent coordinator, Tintin, who ran everything like clockwork.

All ten members of her bridal party felt comfortable with their march and timing. Tintin had them repeat their parts until she thought the timing was just right.

It was choreographed beautifully. The guys marched one at a time then knelt on one knee with one arm set at an angle awaiting their partner with heads bowed. As they waited they gave the impression of concern, as if they were praying they would be picked. As each bridesmaid approached their partnered groomsman, the man quickly jumped to his feet with a transformed expression of victory.

Most of the bridesmaids were friends she had met either at pharmacy school or on the job. Her maid of honor was Maxine, whom she had met at pharmacy school. There were also her dear friend and colleague Rhea, Renee from pharmacy school, her sister-in-law Stephanie, and another dear friend Evette. The best man was Aubyn's brother Dean, and the other groomsmen were her brother Everett, cousins Gary and Kirk-Lance, and a dear friend, Simon.

Everyone rehearsed except her dad, and she hoped he would be able to fit into the beat of the march as he walked her up. He had planned to come up on Sunday so she had known he would not be practicing.

It was after 10 pm when they left the church. Aubyn and Dean, along with her two dear friends Nikki G and Nikki R who were part of the usher team, stayed at the houses of two friends of Aunt Lorraine's.

It was already quite late, and Roberta was getting a bit jittery as she still had ribbons to attach to several baskets. She did not ask for help, but when her aunt stopped by her room she voiced that she wasn't sure when she would be done with the baskets.

Her aunt responded immediately, "My love, you will have to see what you can do because I am exhausted, and I have to get some rest."

Luckily three of her bridesmaids stayed at her aunt's with her and offered to assist. She was up until midnight when her girlfriends told her to get some sleep. Between the three of them they could be done in an hour. She was very happy to have good friends, and she knew her mom would be more than willing to help, but she wouldn't be able to get there until Sunday.

Portmore was known for being too warm and humid. Even during the night she could feel the perspiration running down her back, and she felt her nightgown adhering to her skin. She thought it was lucky her aunt had promised to allow her dress in her bedroom, which was twice the size of her room and the only room in the house equipped with an air conditioning unit. She could not imagine getting dressed in this same room in her long heavy wedding gown with only a rotating fan to help cool her off.

The homes on the island generally were not installed with AC units, but she thought that Portmore should be the exception.

In spite of only getting a few hours' rest she woke up early, and thanks to the adrenaline she did not feel tired. The morning sped on and by 11 am her beautician was there to start her hair and to help with her dress. They started off in the small room, and once again Aunt Lorraine reassured her that Uncle Lou would get dressed soon so she could finish up in the larger and cooler room. Her hair was done, and it was time to get her face done. As the foundation was applied to her face she could feel beads of sweat forming and running down her face. Aunt Lorraine got dressed in another room, but her uncle did not enter the room to be dressed until close to 1 pm. She then knew she would not get the comfort of the room she had been promised as the wedding would start at 2 pm. They made do with the small room, but it was hot and uncomfortable. It took twice as long for the beautician, and she too was complaining of the heat. As fast as she applied the light makeup she patted her face as she continued to perspire and then applied more. There was not much that could be done as the fan was already on high speed. By the time she stepped into the dress she realized just how much of a furnace the room was.

The dress was made of made of lace and satin with sleeves of pure lace. The plush train was about two feet long.

She did not leave the house until two o'clock. The church was less than ten minutes away. She could not rush anymore as she did not want to get any warmer. She was well composed and was feeling confident and happy when Aunt Lorraine told her that the limousine was waiting for her at the front.

She almost gasped when Aunt Lorraine unexpectedly grabbed her and started sobbing. "I am sorry, but I just can't help it. You look so beautiful, and I can't believe it. This is the day we've all been waiting for. Come give your aunt a hug."

Roberta could no longer maintain her composure and wished she could as the light mascara that she had dared to use must have started to look like a mess. Luckily her beautician was there to dab at her face and reapply it.

She was expecting an extended limousine, but it was not. It had cost her quite a lot for the use of the car, and now she wondered how her entire bridal party would fit in it. A middle-aged man dressed in an unfashionable red and white plaid bush jacket held the door ajar as she was assisted inside.

If nothing else worked inside the old limo the air conditioner was a welcomed commodity. It was refreshing. As the old car rolled up the street toward the magnificent church, she hoped the other wedding was done. She just could not tolerate anything else's going wrong.

She was relieved as they approached the church yard. She saw what appeared to be the last set of cars from the one o'clock wedding leaving. She still couldn't understand how Pastor Lewis was able to perform such a ceremony in only an hour, but she was happy he had.

All of her guests and the bridal party were already inside the church. The limousine pulled up at the front of the church, and she was met at the door by her coordinator. She was such a calming presence as she allayed her fears by telling her that her dad was a natural and knew his part.

The church was extremely quiet as she emerged from the car and entered the foyer. She started to read in her very quiet voice words dedicated only to her groom as all turned around in their seats to face her.

She asked for a microphone while still in the foyer and began to speak in a quiet tone: "Aubyn, today I publicly say yes to you. Your personality, your charisma, your warmth have drawn me to you. You are a genuine guy. You are for real, darling.

"I love you, Aubyn. This I hope you will never get tired of hearing. To my new mom and dad, if you had never given me a gift before that would be OK because today you have given me a most precious gift. Thank you, Lord, for this special day."

Her voice was a little shaky and her eyes misty, but her voice was clear for all to hear. As her father met her just before she entered the church, the 250 guests stood and the famous "Here Comes the Bride" rang out from the old pipe organ. It had such a rich sound, and she had requested it especially.

As she walked in the long heavy dress she remembered being told by Tintin to kick as she walked to create a path for her feet and prevent herself from tripping. The walk seemed long and needed much effort. Her dad walked with her until they were halfway up the aisle.

There were several lavender and lime green ribbons tied across the aisle extending from one bench to the other. As Aubyn walked down to meet her she noticed he had been given a pair of scissors as he cut his way across the obstacles to gain access to her. This was both Nikki R's and her coordinator's idea, and she agreed it was quite fitting.

As he took her from her dad, the soloist began to sing in his deep bass, "You by My Side That's How I See Us," by Julia Rogers. She saw a quick exchange between both men, but she didn't hear what was said.

Aubyn had on a sharp-looking dark suite with soft thin stripes and shiny boots to match. He was stunning. On his left breast was pinned a corsage a little larger than the other men's. Her heart skipped a beat, and she gasped as the reality hit that this was indeed happening. He held her gently. He was smiling and looking confident and well-composed, taking care to ensure her dress was not getting in her way.

They approached the arch, and it was gorgeous. She had it designed for the occasion. It had the usual four columns, but they were thick and covered in fluffy white lace interspersed with the wedding colors and wild green ferns. It was an original design she had not seen any like this in any of the catalogues she looked at.

To their left were the four bridesmaids and the maid of honor, and to their right were the groomsmen and the best man. Some of the girls were dressed in off-the-shoulder lavender gowns with matching glittering shawls, while the others were dressed in lime green of exactly the same design. All five gentlemen were smartly clad in black suits with lavender shirts, pocket pieces, and black bowties. In the center on the platform above them were the three officiating ministers: Pastor Bylton, Pastor Lewis, and Pastor Don.

To the right of the ministers was a miniature table with three candles on silver stands. The bride and groom were instructed by Pastor Bylton to hold a lit candle to light up the bigger center candle. Pastor Bylton gave a fifteen minute sermonette as he explained the significance of the candles: "This is the day you demonstrate to all that you are no longer two but one. These are the unity candles."

It was then time for Pastor Don to address them. He directed his conversation to Aubyn first as he had been his pastor since he had been a teen. He then spoke to them both, and he too did a mini-sermon. The mantle was on Pastor Lewis, the Pastor of the Portmore Church, to carry out the exchange of vows.

Pastor Lewis asked the groom, "Do you, Aubyn St. Patrick Sullivan, take Roberta Samantha Swinton to be your lawful wedded wife?"

Roberta heard huge laughter in the church as Aubyn responded with a resounding, "Double yes!"

Pastor Lewis then pronounced them man and wife. There was a loud cheer, and she heard her new mother-in-law, who was seated just two rows from the platform, shout happily, "Done deal!"

Everyone cheered. It was truly a blessed day.

They were led toward the back of the church into Pastor Lewis' vestry as she was going to sign the name "Swinton" for the last time and take on her new name, the name of her dearly beloved.

She heard Momsy singing triumphantly, "Oh, Perfect Love," after she had dedicated it to her son and her new daughter. She was amazed at how well she sang as she did not know of her to sing publicly. The renowned Edward Charles thrilled them with his music as the singing continued.

They emerged in fifteen minutes and received a standing ovation as they were announced by Pastor Lewis as the newest couple in town.

"Please welcome for the first time Mr. and Mrs. Aubyn Sullivan!"

The congregation cheered and applauded loudly.

The bridal party exited before them and formed an arch with their arms, the guys on one side and the ladies on the other, just beyond the one she had designed. As the couple walked through they were pelted with confetti and greeted by their guests.

The door of the limousine was held ajar by the chauffeur as they entered. Aubyn did not know this yet as he had not been driven to church in that car. It was clear the entire bridal party would never fit in the car. Roberta was so worried, not to mention disappointed.

Aubyn whispered to her, "I hate to tell you this, dear, but did you notice the oil leaking from the car?" He laughed. "Don't worry. If you didn't notice maybe no one else will."

As the bridal party tried to get into the limo they too realized they would have to get to the reception area by alternative means. In addition to the couple they were only able to fit two others. The chauffeur's retort still echoed in her head: "You cannot hold. You're going to pop it down!" She could read the fear in their expressions as no one was sure how to make alternative arrangements.

As they drove off she tried not to worry. It would all work out. The Lord surely did not bring them this far to leave them now. Yet as they headed to the hotel there was even more disappointment on the way.

Her aunt had mentioned that there were two ways to get to the hotel and that she would ensure that the procession traveled on the better roadway.

No one expected the limo driver to pick the side road, and of course everyone followed. The road they took brought them past some unsightly sites. They passed fishing villages that had the day's garbage hanging for all to see. It was embarrassing. The road she had hoped they would travel was much more developed and residential and would have been a welcomed difference.

She recalled not being very impressed with the venue. The only thing she had truly liked when she went to look just before the wedding was the ocean in the background. The hotel was too small, and worst of all the reception area was not fully enclosed. Some of the guests were placed in the open area. All the tables were nicely dressed and everyone looked comfortable, but she only prayed it would not rain.

The head table was rather long and seated twelve comfortably, which was a relief. They were still awaiting the arrival of the other eight members, and she hoped it would not be too long before they got there. She prayed that they would come right now before it became obvious. Just as she was praying and hoping, they filed in, arriving just about ten minutes after they did. She was dying to find out how they had made it, but she was sure she would know soon enough. Roberta's cousin Gary, who was just three seats away from her with a mischievous grin and obviously viewing the entire event as a comedy, told her that Pastor Lewis had arranged transportation for the "stragglers."

The evening progressed uneventfully. The guests seemed to be enjoying themselves. There were a number of toasts, but they were humorous and to the point. Dean's speech stood out clearly as Roberta later considered some of his words. He did not even write one. He just spoke.

"I had never planned to share my brother with anyone, but I will share him with you. You guys go together like bread and butter and like ripe banana and condensed milk." By now everyone was doubling over, and there were howls of laughter.

The master of ceremonies said, "I have heard of strange menus in boarding school, but this one gets the award."

Roberta laughed and glanced at Aubyn, and she could see him grinning.

In between the speeches they could hear *cling cling cling* as the glasses were tapped, indicating they wanted to see yet another kiss. They did it so often that she was hoping they would stop.

Phena spoke as well, sounding more like a mini-sermon. "You two, my dear son and Roberta the daughter I never had, I love you with my heart, and I am blessed that my son found you. Remember this day, July 6, 1903."

The guests laughed in good humor and shouted, "2003!"

"Yes, I thank you," she said as she smiled. "Remember this day as you have taken your vows. When the storms come, and they will come, reflect on this day and get through those storms!"

Dims spoke words of exhortation to her daughter and Aubyn in the form of a poem that she had carefully penned. Dims never lacked for words.

It was then the time that they all had waited for. The man of the hour came forth to speak to his guests. Aubyn seemed nervous, and his voice was low. Roberta wished he would speak louder, and thankfully after few moments into his speech he must have become more relaxed as he became more audible and appeared more composed.

She knew from experience and from his own admission that his words didn't always come out right. She had faith in him that he would express himself just the way he intended. As she listened she noticed his message included everyone, both the married and the single.

She heard whispers around the main table where Gary and Everett chanted, "Say the word. Say the word," as he constantly referred to her by her name. Then came an obviously loud sigh of relief as the mischievous Gary and Everett heard him say for the very first time "my wife" as he thanked Roberta and everyone for making the evening a memorable one. Everyone cheered. The event was coming to a close. There was just one last task for her to perform, and the day would be sealed.

A tired but happy-looking Mrs. Sullivan emerged from behind the main table and hurled the bouquet as far as she could as all the young women ran and jumped as if trying to catch "the pearl of great price." It was caught by her long-time high school friend Michelle as she laughed triumphantly. She was always a winner in academics and sports, so this was not much of a surprise.

Both Aubyn and his mom had tried to get her to wear a garter with the intent that he would use his teeth to pull it from off her thigh. She said a vehement, "No!" as there was just no way she would permit that for all eyes to see.

Then it was all over. The day that brought such an array of emotions and required so much time, planning, and coordination had come and ended. The rest of their lives was only partially charted out, and all of it was ahead of them.

They had to be at the Hibiscus Gardens tonight for the start of the honeymoon in St. Ann's, and that was a whopping four-hour ride! Aunt Lorraine and her family had gone there numerous times, and she highly recommended it, and they agreed that would be the venue.

They quickly went by her aunt for her to change into something more comfortable and appropriate as well as to grab a few things. Wayne, who worked at Aunt Lorraine's business as a driver, would be driving Roberta's car for the long trek. She did not realize how hungry she was until they journey started. She had hardly touched her meal at the wedding reception, with all the activity and excitement she had not felt hungry.

Wayne had asked if he could bring a friend so he would have company for the return trip, and they quickly agreed. That turned out to be a drama in itself. He was supposed to be picking up a female companion, but things weren't going as he expected as the exchanges over the phone were not pleasant. He repeatedly apologized as they both pretended not to notice.

Wayne was on the phone constantly, and then about an hour into the journey he asked for a small turn off the road to pick up his friend, but it was not a short turn off. Roberta was beginning to worry as it was pitch dark with no street lights on the path they had taken. The only illumination came from the lights from houses in the distance and the headlights on her car. It was already after 10 pm, and they still had three more hours to go. Finally he stopped at a small house with no sign of life except for a light streaming through a window.

A young lady appeared, apparently coming off the nightshift as she was still in uniform. She was a quiet, pleasant young girl, perhaps about twenty-five. Finally they were on their way again to the resort. Hopefully, there would be no further need to stop along the way as they were both dying to shower and hit the bed.

Aubyn pulled her head against his shoulder, and he laced his fingers through hers as they rode in the back, both silent and exhausted. The two in front seemed to have resolved their differences as they were looking like a happy couple. She smiled to herself as she thought of all the drama that already occurred and could not help wondering what was ahead. All she knew was that she felt confident that it would be all right because God was in this thing, as her mother used to say.

She looked at her watch, and it was just a little after 1 am when Wayne pulled into the resort. It was so brightly lit everywhere that it felt like daylight, and the property seemed like one large garden with several cottages and cobblestones and little streams interspersed throughout. Also, in the quiet of the night they could hear the waves of the ocean beating across the shore, and it seemed to be so close.

Wayne and Aubyn got the luggage, and Roberta checked to ensure they weren't leaving any of their belongings. They were only spending four days and three nights, but they had two huge bags as though they would be spending two weeks. Wayne waited until they got their keys and were checked in before he left.

A friendly gentleman dressed in a sharp uniform from the front desk waved vaguely in the distance and handed them the keys and a map. They got a trolley and loaded up their stuff. After a couple of left turns and then a right, they were in their suite on the second floor with an ocean view.

Being such a gentleman, he offered her the use of the bathroom first. It felt good to be in the shower, and it was so much better when she was all done and dressed in her skimpy little nightdress. It was a leopard print spaghetti strap nightdress that just barely covered her thighs. She had gotten several of these cute little nighties at the engagement party in California and the bridal shower put on by her friends on the island. This one was a gift from her husband's aunt, Aunt Pats.

As she came out of the bathroom, it was very awkward. She felt almost naked so she pulled on the matching robe that was equally short, but at least she felt more clad. He went in the bathroom after her, then she heard him yelling, "Dear, after all that packing can you believe we have no toothpaste?"

She was hoping they would be provided with some, but evidently not. "Are you sure?"

"I was going to have a hot drink then look under the sink as I assume that should be a likely place."

"Are you behind the curtain? I could come in and check right now."

"Yes, I am. But, Roberta, does it really matter if I'm behind the curtain or not? Come on, after all, that's a bit crazy. It's OK, though. I understand that's just probably your way, not a problem."

She thought about it. It was indeed crazy, but just the fact that he said that made her heart beat crazily. He stepped out with only a pair of shorts on and turned all the bright lights off, so she felt way more at ease.

"Well, we have our toothbrushes," he said. "So we will just make do with that and good old water. One night can't hurt. We will be just fine 'til morning, and then we'll get some."

She felt a little irresponsible. She had always taken care of things and couldn't believe she had forgotten toothpaste, although she really had expected that to be provided. She would rather be out of bath soap than toothpaste.

They made do with brushing their teeth and were in bed by 2 am. She did not know when she fell asleep. She didn't even think she wished him goodnight. The last thing she remembered was how loud the waves sounded as they beat on the rocks as she drifted off to sleep.

It must have been her conscience or the urge to use the bathroom, but she jumped up as day was peeping, rolled over to him, and found his eyes wide open.

"I'm so sorry, dear," she said. "I don't know when I fell asleep. I was so tired, and I guess my body wouldn't let me stay up a minute longer."

He lay there just staring at her with those pretty, big, full eyes that she rarely saw as they were usually hidden behind his glasses. She wondered if he had even slept. Did he have something on his mind or feel deserted, she wondered? She surely did not mean to fall asleep like that, but she had been so beat and just fell into a deep slumber. He looked tired last night, so he must have slept too.

He never said a word, just smiled as they lay there and enjoyed intimate moments together. They had waited for so long, getting close, but never close enough. They were filled with anticipation with hearts racing rapidly as their marriage was consummated. It was a beautiful moment, one that Roberta wanted to savor for evermore. Now they were truly one, and he was the other part of her. Only two more nights, and they would be leaving. She wished the days would just stand still or that they could afford to stay an entire week. They had both already spent so much. Excluding Aubyn's portion, Roberta was well into the thousands.

They got up around 11 am. They were famished and decided on calling for room service rather than walking down to the dining room. She ordered ackees and cod fish with crispy, golden brown breadfruit while he ordered a huge omelet and toast with orange juice.

Room service knocked, and the servers led them to the balcony at the back of the suite overlooking the turquoise ocean. It felt like a dream as they ate together on the balcony listening to the sea rushing to shore at a table intended only for two.

After they ate he set the camera timer and quickly ran to her side in order to be caught in the picture along with her. They took several shots together. Afterwards she sat on his lap as they forgot about everything else but that living a fantasy was heavenly.

They really had to get some toothpaste, and right across the street there was a shop much closer than the shopping center. The grounds were gorgeous. She felt she could just sit there and admire it all day. It was so tranquil and relaxing and absolutely beautiful. The maintenance of the grounds was obviously a lot of work as there were so many flowers and lush green plants to nurture.

They returned from the shop and just wanted to do nothing. They headed back to their room and just went back to bed. They enjoyed each other's company so much she was content just to lay there being next to him. As they lay there on the bed they had an easy view of the ocean. The turquoise blue was so captivating and so unreal and must have been reflecting the coral reef below. It looked like a perfect painting.

It was not until close to 6 pm when they dragged themselves up to get ready for dinner. They decided against room service this time. They went into the dining area and were surprised to see how crowded it was. They had planned to sit in the open air anyway to get a good view of the sea. He too loved the view, but he allowed her to lead the way.

As they shared their food and were making their way through the dining area she was sure she saw somebody who looked like Pastor Don. She told her husband, and they took a second glance. It certainly was Pastor Don, as well as what seemed like the entire entourage that had flown out for the wedding. As this was four hours away from the wedding venue, they must have decided to get a hotel on this side instead.

It was quite a coincidence. They could have chosen anywhere in Montego Bay, Negril, Portland, for instance. Momsy and Dean were also there, and Roberta smiled as she saw the familiar faces but couldn't disguise her surprise. Momsy explained that her friend June who flew down with her had a brother who owned a beach front lodge in St. Ann's and they all decided to spend the time there. There were still several other places to dine, but she figured that explained it. They were staying in St. Ann's and just happened to be dining at the Hibiscus.

Pastor Don's wife started to scoot them out of the dining area. "You guys, go, go, go. You should not be wasting time with us. You need to be enjoying each other."

With no further ado Roberta led the way to a secluded little spot with dim lighting in the open air. It was a little chilly, but it was fine as they both had on light jackets.

It was around 8 pm when they leisurely made their way back to their room. Hand in hand they walked, which was quite unusual for her. It felt good. They even became a little adventurous as he decided to explore the grounds a little. She was always the cautious type and preferred to stick to what she knew. She only knew the one path back so far and certainly would not be able to find her way back without him now that they had deviated from it, she thought.

The way they walked took twice as long, but it did not matter as they were in no hurry. There was no paperwork to get done, no chores to do. It was just timeless and blissful, and it was too bad, she thought, that it would soon come to an end, and it would be back to reality. She decided not to worry about that and basked in the moment at hand.

Tuesday morning came so quickly, and they would be leaving the next day. She suddenly realized that they had slept together for two nights already, and she had not heard him snore. She remembered when she had heard him snore that one time in her apartment and wondered if she could ever sleep in the same room with him. It seemed as though she wasn't going to be bothered by it after all. It was either that he only snored sometimes or she tuned it out when she slept. *That's just great,* she thought.

It was around 10 am when there was a knock on their door. They did not call for room service and were getting ready to head down for breakfast. They did not get the door immediately because the knock was so faint.

There was a second knock, and Aubyn called out, "Just a minute!"

When he opened the door, Roberta was shocked and wondered if everything were all right. It was his mother at the door.

She stepped inside and asked Roberta, "How is married life, Mrs. Sullivan?"

Roberta responded with a puzzled, "Good."

Her mother-in-law then shot back, "It better be."

Roberta was expecting to hear that something had happened or that there was an emergency and Phena had no choice but to see them, but it soon became clear Momsy was simply visiting them on day two of their honeymoon. It was a bit unsettling, and she felt self-conscious as their bed was not made and they were definitely not expecting anyone.

"You guys got a nice room," Phena said. Aubyn then led her through the room to the balcony where she exclaimed that she loved the view. She explained that she was close by and thought she would drop in.

"It was so hard to find you guys, and the front desk people were so difficult. They would not give any information. After explaining who I was and that it was important that I see you guys, then they did."

She only stayed for about fifteen minutes. Roberta felt some compassion for her. She was not sure as to the cause, but she detected some sadness. They hugged her, and she left.

Alone with her new husband, she could not help asking Aubyn if he thought his mother were OK and voiced her concerns that she did look troubled. He brushed it off.

"You'll soon understand my mom. She is always worrying about stuff, even stuff she can't control. Who knows what she is bothered by this time?

She will be all right. She is a tough woman. God knows the things I have seen her go through, and she always comes out all right. Anyway, let's get some food 'cause you know I have a healthy appetite, and I could really use some food now before my blood sugar gets any lower."

They ate and decided to check out the beach. They sat on the sea shore together, heads leaning close, staring at the ocean and taking in the fresh air as they threw little pebbles into the water. She so badly wanted to feel the water on her, and she went straight in wearing just what she had put on for breakfast, a close-fitting pair of jeans shorts and a knitted light green shirt.

"Come on, Aubyn," she called. "Get in! It feels great in here."

He jumped in, and it was such fun even though he too was not dressed for the beach. It really did not matter; it was fun. After a while Roberta saw a huge log in the water and climbed up to perch on it. She loved taking pictures to capture every moment, and she loved having her picture taken especially. There was an old boat nearby, and they posed next to that also. The water felt nice and warm as the afternoon sun shone brilliantly. The climate was just right. It was not hot although the water was warm as they could feel a gentle breeze.

Time passed so quickly they must have spent over three hours there. He eventually beckoned to her that they should be heading back now. He said he just wanted to get back to their room, shower, and relax in bed. She too agreed that she would enjoy jumping back in bed.

They showered and before long were relaxing in bed again with him flipping through the television channels as they snuggled up close with her head resting on his chest. She opened all the windows. It was very private as the only thing behind their room was the big wide ocean. As she looked through the window and thought about how she just loved being in the water and how she was surely going to miss being able to gaze at it. This must be the Pisces in her speaking out.

She ran out of bed feeling the urge to urinate, and he asked, "Are you OK, dear? You just went a few minutes ago."

"I am fine, but I keep wanting to go, and when I go I feel like I cannot completely void."

The rest of the evening into night was the same thing. She enjoyed the time spent. She loved the hotel and knew she would have memories for many more years, but it was getting uncomfortable, so she was relieved that they would be leaving the next day.

"Sorry if I'm not much fun right now," she said. "But I am sure it will be OK. As soon as we return I will see my doctor." She got up at least five times that night.

"Well, Sweetie, it could be worse. At least this was not happening when we just got here. This is the eve of going home, so it's OK, really."

She hugged him, thinking he was so sweet and understanding, and she felt blessed that he was that type of guy.

They were up around 8 am and called room service for breakfast. They ate on their balcony and enjoyed the few hours they had left as they inhaled the sea breeze and listened to the water rushing to shore.

They had to be checked out before midday, so they therefore started packing right after breakfast. After they packed she went back and double-checked to ensure that neither of them was leaving personal belongings behind. Luckily she was always double-checking everything, she thought, as she did find one of her slippers on the floor that had managed to make its way out of her luggage.

They were done and in the lobby by 11:30 am awaiting Wayne's arrival for the trip back to Portmore. After that journey they would soon be heading back to her apartment in Mandeville. He was there by 11:45 am, and then they were on their way back. Wayne was playing the role of tour guide as he pointed out historic and important sites to Aubyn as they went by. Both men talked on the way back as they got more acquainted, but she was quiet and pensive.

They decided to stay overnight at Aunt Lorraine's and return to Mandeville the next day. It was a bit late, and they wanted to see Aubyn's father anyway.

That night at Aunt Lorraine's they were told they would be staying in the same room that Roberta had dressed in for the wedding. That room had twin beds, and interestingly enough her aunt went through the trouble of putting both beds together.

Aubyn did not care for that and told her, "Roberta, it's weird for us to sleep in the same bed in their house. I think I will use another room."

"Aubyn, I think it would be weird if we didn't because that's expected. I don't feel weird at all."

"Guess it's the old fashioned me talking now," he said. "It's just that I respect them so much and just days earlier we couldn't and now we can, and I thought, let's save that until we get to your place."

"Believe me, both she and Uncle Lou would be worried if we didn't. They would wonder what happened on the honeymoon, and they would have every right to, don't you think?"

"I see what you're saying, and now that you explained it that way I guess you're right," he said.

CHAPTER 8:
THE SEPARATION

t was all over. The wedding had passed, and they had their entire lives ahead of them. It was four whole days since the wedding, and she found it hard to believe.

They arrived at her apartment around midday Thursday. They had no plans to do anything as they were feeling the toll of the drive as well as all the preceding events. They were both looking forward to staying in and making an early start on Friday as he would be returning to the States that Sunday. She noticed he proceeded to the room that had been his ever since he first came to her place. He soon returned with his things and grinned at her.

"I dreamt of sleeping in this bed ever since last week when I got here, and now I figure I am worthy to do so. Ready or not, here I come."

She had lived at this apartment for two years and never shared her bed, so she found it strange to share it with her husband for at least the next three nights. She did not want to think that in a matter of days he would be gone, and she would be alone once more. Roberta was still experiencing the frequent urination, although the discomfort had subsided. She decided she would pay her doctor a visit that same day, although she much preferred staying in with her husband. She told him she would be right back, but he volunteered to accompany her.

Her doctor told her that the symptoms she was experiencing was very common for new brides and the diagnosis was "honeymoon cystitis." She smiled at the thought and was thankful it was not more serious. He prescribed to her a short course of antibiotics and added that as the novelty wore off she would no longer encounter that problem.

She slept deeply that night. He had already learned her usual sleeping position. She felt so secure snuggling in his arms with her head on his chest. Aubyn usually turned facing her with one arm across her waist. It was interesting that although she thoroughly liked snuggling up, she had to be free of the embrace to accomplish sleep. He too had his way. When he fell asleep he generally had his right hand resting on his left breast almost in a protective manner. How much she had learned in only a few days.

On Friday morning they drove down to Little Ochie and picked a spot in one of the old boats with thatch roof. It was creatively renovated with steps and seating into a quaint dining area. It seated six around the makeshift table, but only the two of them were there.

He liked any view with the sea as a backdrop, just as she did. It had to be the Pisces in both of them. This was a place that served only seafood, but he wanted to come here anyway as he had heard so much about it.

He held her. "It will be OK, dear. I'm a big boy now. It's just that ever since Dean had his nightmare I have just avoided it. Promise, I'll be super careful."

They ordered, and she took care to suggest that he try the jack fish as it had fewer bones to contend with. He wanted to venture after so many years of abstaining, and she did not want him to regret it.

They ate with thankfully no mishaps. He was apprehensive at first as he tried a bit of the fish and then became more confident. He got through the bammies and festival in no time. So she had no doubt the meal was great. Roberta was fascinated as she heard him singing along with Bob Marley's music. *Baby don't worry about a thing cause every little thing is gonna be all right.* This guy had not been to the island in years, and she was impressed that he knew the lyrics.

The meal, the atmosphere, the scenery, the music, and the company were truly fine. They lingered quite a while after the meal. Neither wanted the moment to end. It was still early in the day, and it felt like honeymoon all over as they held hands and gazed into each other's eyes, not saying much. They both knew that it was a tough road ahead, and they wanted to cherish the moments as that was all they would be left with for a long time.

He wanted to see a little more of Alligator Pond in Manchester where Little Ochie was located. It was only 1:07 pm, so she said, "Yes, I could drive around for a while in the vicinity." She did not want to venture too far as there were miles of empty land and ocean as far as they could see.

The people in the area led a simple life, depending mainly on fishing and farming. There were few very large homes and many smaller ones. The life looked peaceful and stress-free away from the city's hustle and bustle. Several people were walking along the road pleasantly greeting the neighbors as they passed with no apparent rush. It was different from Mandeville. Mandeville was a lovely clean town, but there was hustle and bustle.

"Wow," he said. "Am I going to miss this. It's such a getaway being here. I mean, not just here but the island on the whole. When I go back it will be so different."

"I know," she said.

"There are so many things I have in mind to accomplish, and will be pushing hard when I return. I have such a zeal now, not like I didn't have before, but now it's just so much more."

He had been laid off since 2000 and was basically working on contract with a company in Upland and had at least three days guaranteed. He also knew this guy from Indonesia, Thein, which had his own business in LA. He had called him a few times. Thein told him that several of the clients requested Aubyn by name and spoke highly of him. Thein called him at least once per week and at times up to three times per week as the jobs were available.

They had to head back. It was still early afternoon, only an hour drive to Mandeville, so they would be back by 3 pm if they left now. Roberta wanted to get some goodies for him to take back home. She stopped in Mandeville and got a few items. She also stopped in one of the local supermarkets and got cassava snacks and green banana and plantain chips that he really liked. Her friend Mrs. Johnson had gotten them plantain tarts that they picked up on the way back.

All that remained to be done was to assist him with packing. They would do the final packing Saturday night except for the freezer items. Those could be packed Sunday morning just before he left.

Just as she feared, Sunday arrived in no time and before long they were at the airport waving good-bye. Sammy drove them to the airport. Her brother Everett and her mother were also there to see him off.

The expression on his face when they hugged and said good-bye was etched in her mind. He wore a black leather jacket, and his face that was normally smiling and pleasant was stony, drawn, and heartbreaking as she tried to maintain her own composure.

Roberta and her family watched until he went through immigrations, and they could still see him going all the way down the long passage. Roberta looked until she could see him no more, but he never looked back.

There was no point in waiting any longer, so they decided to leave right away. Dims knew he would not be flying for two hours. "I think we should wait a while longer just to ensure there are no delays or cancellations. I have had the experience before so, believe me, I know," said Dims.

They understood, but decided to be on their way anyway as Everett reminded her that they had checked the monitors and the flight would depart on time. He joked to his mother, "The geezer is at it again. Prophet of doom and gloom, can't you be positive for once and trust God it will be all right? By the way, we are leaving, so let us know if you want us to return for you tomorrow."

Everyone tried to create a light mood during the drive back home, but Roberta didn't feel like saying much. She was fine just quietly reflecting, apparently in her own world.

The return trip felt longer than the trip to the airport. She was just glad when she was finally home. She didn't have to talk if she didn't feel like it as she was back at her place by herself. Everett was first dropped off at his house, then her mom who lived about half an hour from her brother.

It was all over now, Roberta thought. The bliss was gone. It was back to work tomorrow and back to real life too. He was still in the air. It was 7 pm her time, which meant it would only be 5 pm California time, and he was not scheduled to arrive at LAX before 9 pm. He had at least another four hours up there. She would hear from him in the morning. She knew he would get home safely because they had both prayed about that.

She just was not in the frame of mind to return to work. She knew there would be a lot of questions, and she was not looking forward to that. She made herself go to work the next day and could not wait to get home to get on her computer. Every time she sat by her computer she was more grateful for it as it made her feel connected to him, and he did not seem that far after all. All it required was for her to get online and dial him. Once his PC was up, even if he were not at his computer at the time, he would notice her trying to reach him and respond.

She was glad to learn his trip was hassle-free. They talked for such a long time until she said, "I should go shower now, and do you know I have not had a bite? I pretty much went right to the computer when I got home."

"You poor dear. Oh no, go eat, Sweetie. We can always talk later if you'd like, but go take care of yourself first," he told her.

She was content knowing she had heard from him, and she was sure after she took care of a couple things they would be talking again that very night. The days and the weeks seemed to run into each other. There were so many things that had to get done, before she joined him so she just wanted the time to go by. She just knew she would have to accomplish everything or time would certainly pass her by.

They talked every day. They both were quite busy and adjusted to the fact that this was normal for them. They complained less about the distance between them. One day he called her as usual and was very excited. She was dying to hear what had excited him so.

"Dear, I got in! I got in. I got accepted!" he blurted out.

"Did you get back into a full-time position with a firm?" she asked, puzzled

"No, I got into the technician program. You know, the one I was telling you about, so I will have a backup when my computer field is not as forthcoming as I would like. That's called job security, girl."

"That's great, Aubyn. I am happy you got in. So when do you start? How long is the program?"

"Sweetie, it is a one-year program. I will have the opportunity to work with the state. It starts this September, and by August 2004 I will be graduating! It will be so different from my current field as now I will be doing psychology, and I am truly looking forward to that."

Roberta had been a registered pharmacist since 1997 and a member of PSJ, a professional organization in her country. Although she had six years' experience in her career when she graduated, they only awarded the diploma in pharmacy. It was shortly after she graduated that the school of pharmacy transitioned into awarding the bachelor's degree in pharmacy, which meant she too needed to return to school to be upgraded. Her program had also been only one additional year.

She had been motivated and decided to pursue the bachelor's degree for the following year. She knew it would be very competitive as there were several of her colleagues from her class and previous classes that wanted to do the upgrade.

She had already heard that it was not a piece of cake getting in. There was limited space, and there were several that wanted the opportunity. All were qualified for the program, and as a result the process of elimination was a panel of three delivering tough questions. Some of her friends made it past the interview while some did not. She knew she had some preparation to do if she were going to be selected. Now more than ever it was important for her to achieve this degree as she would be immigrating someday to join her husband.

Aubyn soon started the program, and he enjoyed the psychology aspect tremendously. But he did not bargain for the tricky quizzes that would be a part of the package. He called her one evening at an all-time low.

"You will not believe this, Sweetie, but I studied real hard, and I failed the quiz. I passed the first one like I told you but messed up real bad on this one."

"Maybe while we talk we could go over some of the lectures together, and I could quiz you," she suggested.

"I told my mom that I messed up again, and she said we need to talk less so that I can study more." He sighed.

"Messed up again? But you said you passed the first one pretty well, and you failed this one, so what do you mean you 'messed up again'?"

"Yeah, I didn't tell you, Hon, but so far I had three quizzes, and I missed two. I passed the very first one."

"That's OK. We can make that a priority. We will go over stuff first, and how about I quiz you after we review?"

He told her that he was doing lots of terminology that sounded very similar and the questions were tricky. He told her the list, and she asked about them in no particular order repeatedly until she was comfortable it had stuck with him. She even made questions for him with fill-in-the-blanks, and she was confident that his next test would be a breeze. She reviewed with him until she really had to tell him goodnight as it was already 10 pm her time.

One night as they started their review, as was now the norm, she heard Momsy in the background. "Say hi to Roberta, but you guys really need to realize you can't be spending so much time talking when you have to prepare for your test."

She was not sure what he said to her, but Roberta did not hear her in the background after that. "Aubyn," she said. "I hope you told her we have been spending most of our time every time we talk reviewing your notes. I really don't want to be blamed for what I'm not responsible for."

"I told her. No need to be bothered about that," he reassured her.

She felt like she knew the material herself and could very well take some of the tests. It was rewarding, though, to study with him and to see his confidence in the material increase.

As the months went by he passed his tests. He had minor hiccups on some new material, but she was pleased when the results came out. Sometimes he passed by not a large margin, but all that mattered was he understood the material enough to pass.

Her interview for entry into the bachelor of pharmacy program came and went, but she would not learn of the results for another two weeks. She felt quite confident as she made questions for herself and he coached her. She found out he had great talent in that area. She hoped she got accepted. If she didn't it would mean a longer time for her to join her husband.

Things were going well. He liked his course, his grades were decent, and she got the letter of acceptance for her program. He was even unanimously selected as class president. His graduation would be in August 2004, and her program would start in September 2004.

It did not seem like a year had passed, but she was soon preparing to take a trip to attend his graduation. She was so happy for him. Now he had an alternative to his primary field. However, the air fare would be expensive, and Roberta was already paying for her car, rent, and utilities.

She was also still paying for her braces and saving for the large school fees. She had been scouting around for reasonable fares and could only come up with prices around US$800 as it was tourist season.

Ever since she had started working she saved religiously every month. She had a heart for charity and occasionally assisted a children's home in her hometown with both her time and what little financial help she could. However, it was posing a strain with so many additional expenses.

She truly contemplated whether she could afford to take the trip. Then she wondered how he would feel if she did not make the effort. She did not want to ask for his assistance, and he was in school full time anyway. She has always paid her own air fares, but now it was just so much going on in quick succession.

She had also just assisted her mother in adding an apartment to her existing home. She had encouraged her mom to do this as this could be a rented property that would bring in income when she retired. She did not anticipate its costing so much, and it did take a chunk from her small savings. She truly felt squeezed, but she knew that God usually saw her through.

She wanted an elegant dress for the occasion. She had never applied for a credit card, so it would also be coming out of her limited budget. Her mom went with her that weekend to a few stores.

After stopping at several stores and not finding anything, they spotted a simple but cute off-the-shoulder, earth-colored dress with an abstract design. It was a lovely dress, but not quite what she was looking for. They were getting tired of not finding what she wanted, and since there was not too much time and this was elegant in its own right she settled on it. It was not a cheap dress either.

Her mom noticed she liked the dress but was not too excited about it, so she told her, "Let's check one other store, and if you see something you like better just return this one."

They went to Midway Mall, and instantly a classy off the shoulder black dress caught her eye. It had three different layers with a unique slant cut exposing one knee and covering the other. Each of the three tiers was trimmed with a rose pink border. She knew this was the dress and was not leaving without it. Her mom said "wow" when she saw it, but also asked the question, "Girl, did you see the price?"

She did, and it was pricy.

When they returned home her mom told her, "I am coming with you to Aubyn's graduation."

"It's expensive, and with everything going on I think you might be putting yourself into too much expense right now," she replied.

"Let's say the excitement rubs off, and besides, that's my son. I have to see him take his award."

Roberta only hoped her mother knew what she was doing, but she could see her mind was made up, and she was aware of how impulsive her mother could be at times.

It was August 6, 2004, and Roberta and her mom were in Raleigh Heights at the house where Aubyn and his family lived. They arrived just two days before the graduation. Roberta was amazed at how much he still had to accomplish as the class president and wondered if his vice president played any role at all. He was constantly dashing out or making phone calls, and she thought to herself, *He will be relived for more reasons than one in the next two days.*

The day came, and she felt overdressed. The venue was in an average size auditorium, and as they walked in several people were dressed in shirt and jeans. Then as others were filing from across the parking lot in the opposite direction she saw a handful of people dressed in elegant evening wear like herself, and that was a relief.

It was well attended, and they were glad for that. Everyone worked hard and deserved the support. The chairperson gave the format of the proceedings. Each graduate was limited to inviting two persons onto the stage and would issue a bouquet to each.

It was finally his turn to take the stage, and as she heard his calm, quiet voice over the speakers her heart swelled with pride. He said, "I want to thank my wife and my mom for the support and the rest of my family. At this time I would like to present this bouquet to my lovely wife, whose patience and support have been my inspiration."

As she walked down the stairway, taking extreme caution not to trip on her long dress, he met her halfway and walked her onto the stage for the presentation. They did a short embrace, and it was time to welcome the next person.

He welcomed his mom next, and Roberta could see that Momsy was taking way too long to get down. The flight of stairs was poorly lit and was potentially unsafe. Aubyn met his mom apart of the way also and escorted her down. After the presentation Roberta, who was still at the bottom of the stairs, held her mother-in-law's hand as they walked slowly back to their seats.

Aubyn's four other guests were: Dean, Rupert, Aunt Noreen, and Dims. As she approached her seat and looked in her mom's direction she could tell from her expression that she was upset. She did not say anything because she was waiting for her mom to talk when she was ready.

When they were exiting the room, her mom began to vent. "Imagine! I traveled several miles to get here, and I was not even acknowledged. Even if I was not called unto the platform, he could have acknowledged me."

Roberta tried in vain to explain that there was a limit of two persons so perhaps after he presented his two bouquets he did not think making mention of anyone else would have been OK. There was also a time constraint.

She knew her mom could be irrational at times because she had had her own experience with her mom. She really hoped she would not be unpleasant to Aubyn when he joined them as, knowing him, he did not intentionally mean to upset her.

Momsy also was displeased, and the mood of the evening was looking sour. This should have been a celebration of his achievement, and there was so much disquiet brewing.

She heard Momsy grumbling, "I would prefer if I was not mentioned. His Aunt Noreen has been through the program before him and has been a resource for him. Aubyn should have never left her out."

Aunt Noreen said, "It's OK, Phena. Really, it's fine. Let him enjoy the day. It's his day, and let him recognize whoever he will."

Roberta truly feared that he was going to walk into all the unrest totally oblivious to what was going on, and that would just ruin everything. He would be so puzzled that he was the target of the entire thing.

Just as she imagined, he did. His mom was reprimanding him, and he got the cold shoulder from Dims. Aunt Noreen and Roberta tried to steer the conversation to what should have been the focus, but the tension was obvious.

Aunt Noreen bid everyone good-bye and went to her car. Aubyn, who needed to be on site before everyone else, drove his car, so Roberta rode back home with him. The others drove back in his mom's van.

On the way home Aubyn kept beating himself up that he wished he had thought of mentioning her mom. "Guess she is so upset with me that she will never talk to me again, right?" He smiled sheepishly.

"Believe me, she will get over it. Trust me, I know," she reassured him.

"Yeah, I'm sure she will be OK," he agreed.

Roberta and her mother were staying for only ten days. Dims and Phena were meeting only for the second time, and both women acted like they had been friends for ages. They had so much in common. They even seemed to enjoy similar jokes. Phena and Dims both were shopaholics and liked to be up and about driving the streets.

Roberta was glad that both women were comfortable with each other, and she did not have to worry about her mother-in-law's trying to persuade her to come out with her on a daily basis.

Roberta and Aubyn thankfully spent lots of time together. He told her that he would be busier than ever after she left as he would be working in both his primary and secondary fields as much as possible.

As they spent the next few days together, he told her the plans he had in mind, and she admired his ambitious dreams. She did hope he was not planning to overdo anything at the expense of adequate rest.

"I am going to be busting my butt, Hon," he said. "I have so many dreams. You just don't know. And I have the vision and drive now. My first task is to purchase a home. I was thinking about our staying at my mom's when you came up, but I remember you saying you did not want to, and I respect that."

She explained, "Your mom is OK. I love your mom. I hope you understand that, but I just think as adults there will be a better relationship when we live apart. I have seen some of that in my own family, and I just want to prevent any problems."

She was happy to know that Aubyn and her mom were joking and teasing each other again. It was great seeing that because the tension was unpleasant. She noticed he first tried more than once to joke with her and she pretended to ignore him. He did not give up until she gave in and blurted, "Leave me alone. I'm not talking to you, man, after the way you treated me." Dims could not help herself she started laughing when he wrapped his arms around her neck from behind while she was seated on a chair.

The trip turned out to be a good one in spite of some of the drama that unfolded. They were seen off at the airport by Aubyn and his mom, and before long they were on the flight home. It gave her a feeling that she was quite familiar with by now.

There was no time to mope or whine. He made it clear he was going to be extremely busy, and she would start school in a matter of just weeks. The time would fly by she was sure of that. She knew there were so many things to look forward to, and things were going in the right direction.

It was a huge transition. She resigned from her fulltime job to return to pharmacy school to do the additional year for the bachelor's. It was a scary step. She would no longer receive a paycheck, and after paying her school fee she was certain what remained would not last too long. She had notified the landlord a month in advance and had already started putting her stuff into boxes.

Two of her colleagues, Irene and Sophia, would be starting the program as well. That was comforting. At least they could study and hang out together. She thought of renting a place close to school off Old Hope Road to avoid spending much time in traffic, like she did years earlier when she did the diploma in pharmacy.

She said this to Aunt Lorraine, who disagreed immediately. "There is no way I could live here in Portmore and have you stay elsewhere for school. Portmore is normally a forty-five minute ride to the university, but with traffic it could be over two hours. But if you leave an hour early you'll avoid the morning traffic congestion."

It sounded like a plan, but Roberta hoped she made the right decision as the places close to school went really fast. Her friend Sophia got a nice flat just fifteen minutes' walk time from school, and there were several in line for the same place. She braced herself as she now pondered the thought of resuming school full time and being jobless.

CHAPTER 9:
THE SEPARATION INTENSIFIED THE CHALLENGES

She arrived at her aunt's house on Sunday, just the day before school started. Roberta and Aunt Lorraine agreed on a monthly figure and they both seemed to be comfortable with that. "Your aunty wishes she did not have to take this from you, but you know the economy," she said.

"That's OK, Aunt Lorraine. I surely would not be comfortable staying here without covering my own expenses."

"It will work out great for you too, Roberta, because when you are on holidays you don't have to give me money for the entire month. I will calculate it based on the time you are actually here."

School started at 8 am, so to be absolutely sure she would not encounter traffic she left at 5:30 am. She was at school by 6:15 and gladly waited in the parking lot where she grabbed her devotional quarterly and read. Before long, Irene pulled up with Sophia. They apparently thought like she did or it might have been just anticipation.

The first day was mainly orientation where it was outlined that this was an accelerated program, and in order to succeed it was imperative that everyone make every day count. There would be surprise quizzes and midterm tests with an emphasis on essays. Course work would include presentations, and there would be quite a bit of research required.

It was no joke, it was a lot of work. The lectures were two to three hours long. In addition to bulky reading packets, there was also quite an amount of note taking. One part-time lecturer who was also the director of a large pharmaceutical company told her class that the key to success was to ensure that all lecture notes are read within the first twenty-four hours for maximum retention. This was definitely going to be one of her goals, Roberta thought, but its feasibility was totally another thing.

She was not hearing from Aubyn much anymore as her aunt no longer had Internet service and it was costly for either of them to call directly. He had become such an integral part of her life, and transitioning from those frequent chats to not at all was agonizing.

She found herself stopping at the library with her two friends when she had class until 5 pm, to avoid peak traffic hour. Sophia also invited them over to study at times as she had access to the Internet.

Roberta found herself driving home quite late as the work got more intense, even as late as after 11 pm sometimes. Her mom called at times and was worried sick that she was still traveling that late, and she knew it was unsafe also. She knew she had to cut into her already tight budget to get an Internet connection. That way she could do her research papers without getting home late. She would also be able to contact Aubyn whenever she could.

She was already four months into the program. After she gave Aunt Lorraine her monthly amount she still had to ensure she had enough for fuel for her car. She bought her own snacks and juices, so she had to have money for that also. She wondered if she had made the right choice because Sophia told her that with only few hundred dollars more she could have gotten a place close to her. Sophia had a small space, so rooming with her was not an option, and the other places were already gone.

Roberta was running low on finances, but she did not want to ask her husband for help just yet. She was planning to work a few hours when her next set of assignments and quizzes were done. One day her aunt went to check the mailbox and handed Roberta an envelope. Her heart skipped a beat. It was from her mother-in-law.

Momsy rarely had time to write letters. She was also quite generous, and so Roberta had no doubt a gift was enclosed. She called infrequently, and Roberta never told her she needed assistance. She tore open the letter and was not disappointed. There in Momsy's handwriting was a check of US$300. Roberta cried literal tears that flowed down her cheeks. Neither Aubyn nor his mom was aware of any difficulties she was having, yet the check was perfect timing.

She called her mom right away and told her of the blessing she just received. She would be calling Momsy that same afternoon as well to let her know how grateful she was.

She weighed all her options. Safety was a priority, and there were several online resources she had to access for success. She probably had enough savings to get her through maybe another four months if she were lucky.

When she talked with her mom about her concerns, she would always tell her the familiar words that she came to believe through experience: "God will provide. I also have been saving in a 'partner draw' with your Aunt Lorraine, and every month a member gets his draw. My draw will be coming up in three months, so I will tell her tonight to give mine to you so finances will not be so tough."

"Mommy, I don't want you to do that," she said. "Trust me. If I have to miss two days at school and go to work I will and catch up on the notes later. You know the hospital pharmacy usually wants a relief person."

"Girl, I tell you the truth. If you don't need all at least I'll give you half. After all, you have always helped me, and I know you always will if I need it."

Roberta felt a weight lifted from her. It was remarkable. It was going to be OK, and she would not have to miss her class deliberately just to make ends meet. She would talk to her sister Lorraine that night and confirm how the payout would be.

Her mom called her on her way from school the following evening just as she got in as if she had timed her somehow.

"I hardly slept last night," she began. "Imagine, I explained to Lorraine that I am depending on that partner draw to help you out, and she told me she will be cancelling it because it is stressing her out and meant to tell me."

Roberta remembered that there were several other people depending on it. There was a single mother who worked as a beautician who depended on the draw every year, and there were at least a dozen others.

"Why now? She has been doing this for five years at least. What was her reason?"

"Well, she said she is tired of reminding and chasing after people to pay on time, and she has to put her health first because she can't afford for anything to stress her to death and cause her to leave her children."

"I even asked her how you will manage and if she could just hold on for just this year since this was so sudden that there were no other arrangements."

She knew her aunt. When she made up her mind she was not going to back down. It was final.

Dims continued, "I'm so sorry, Roberta, but like I say, God always provides. Believe me, I begged and pleaded on your behalf, but she was as tough as a rock, not budging.

"By the way, did you get the paperwork from the registrar in Spanish Town that you needed to send to Aubyn?"

"God is great! I was asking Sophia and Irene if they knew of a place closer where I could get the certificates rather than going to Spanish Town, and they said there was one off Old Hope Road on the way to the university.

"Mommy, would you believe I got there before seven in the morning, and they were open at 7:30? I was out in fifteen minutes.

Roberta had a tight time frame within which to return the preliminary documents to her husband. Her school schedule was posing a challenge, and she could not pick a suitable day to skip school without missing out on important lectures. Spanish Town was guaranteed to have traffic. When she learned of an alternative, the relief was tremendous.

She remembered mentioning the problem to her aunt, not really asking but hoping for assistance.

"Roberta," Aunt Lorraine had said, "my dear, I just went there last month for your Uncle Lou, and I will have to go there again next month with your cousin. I cannot go there now. I am busy at the office. If you can't take time from school, then you will have to ask Dims to come and do that for you."

Roberta recalled thinking that her mom, who did not drive, would have to travel over two hours on public transportation to get there. She had been faced with having to find a way somehow.

"Aunt Lorraine," she had said. "It's fine. Don't worry about it. I will figure it out. I could never put my mother through that. In fact, if I have to miss a class to do it I would prefer that to asking Mommy."

She thought of how overwhelmed and alone she felt at that point. There was the pressure of school, financial challenges, and completing immigration paperwork, and she had just longed to be with her honey where she could feel loved, pampered, and spoiled. She longed to have secure arms to fall into so she did not feel she had to bear it by herself.

Roberta had passed all the quizzes so far, and though the research papers were a challenge they were coming along. She had already completed two midterms. She had gotten an A on one and just barely missed getting a B on the other. Her hopes were so dashed, and the next month was fast approaching where she had to pay the amount agreed upon to her aunt. She still had that amount to give her, but she needed to replenish her funds soon.

That same evening Roberta called one of the hospital pharmacies that she used to work at part time and told them she would be available Thursday and Friday of the following week.

Her friend Eva was the pharmacy manager and was glad to oblige. She was actually looking to get few days off and did not have a replacement. She told Roberta she would have preferred a week later, but was happy for any help at all.

Roberta knew missing an actual lecture for any class would make it difficult to catch up, and just getting the notes were no substitute for the class. At least the classes she was most concerned about, namely Therapeutics and Pharmaceutical Chemistry, were not scheduled on those days.

The other issue was telling her friends she would be absent next Thursday and Friday without conveying too much information. The truth was all this time since she started this program she hadn't worked because her school schedule was intense, which left her little time. However, being this low and funds didn't leave her much choice. Sophia and Irene were great friends, but perhaps due to pride Roberta did not want them to know the reason for her missing school.

That would be a task because they could read her like a book. She'd probably tell them over the phone so they could not see her expression. Then she could end the call quickly.

As planned, she worked Thursday and Friday as a relief at the hospital, and she knew her check would be in the mail within a week. She did not bargain on seeing "Mr. T," as the drug rep was affectionately called. Of course, he sent his regards to Irene and Sophia, which she accepted but had no intention of delivering as that would pose more questions from the girls. She smiled at the thought.

Monday as usual she arrived at school early and shortly after the other two showed up.

"Miss Roberta, come here, Little Missy," said Irene with her characteristic chuckle.

Roberta's brows furrowed. They never called her "Miss Roberta," especially not in that tone. She glanced at Sophia, and her expression was just like Irene's.

"Miss Roberta?" she echoed

"That's surely what I said," repeated Irene while Sophia nodded, pretending to be serious.

"So you were at the hospital working two days for Eva," Irene stated trying in vain to be serious.

"What?" asked Roberta.

"Yes, so I guess that was the emergency and the reason you couldn't be in class and had to rush off the phone like you did. Do you know how concerned we were, Missy? Sophia and I said, 'That's not like Roberta.'"

"I didn't say it was an emergency," she said, feeling cornered and a bit silly. She was sure that Eva had let the cat out of the bag.

Sophia, who usually didn't speak much, said, "Well, you surely acted like it, Roberta. We are your friends, dear. You could have told us. I might as well tell you how we heard. I went down to Mandeville Friday after class, and I stopped by my old workplace. There was Mr. T. He was so excited to see me. Of course, he had no idea your trip was a sworn secret, so that's how that went."

"So you see, Missy, when you plan this again you might as well tell us 'cause we have a way of finding out. Right." winked Irene.

At that point Roberta let them know she really did not have much choice. Both girls who have always been supportive to her empathized with her but asked that she levels with them if there is a reoccurrence.

Everything was happening so rapidly. Aubyn called to let her know that escrow had closed on the home he bought.

She was elated. "Our own home," she said. "I wish I were there to be a part of it. When I come up and find a job at least you will have help." It was a promise.

His aunt had a nice four-bedroom house in Santa Clementa that she was selling to move to another city. She wondered why his aunt was moving out, and she had heard that it was not the greatest area. Roberta prayed he made the right choice when he purchased the house.

She remembered when her dad had purchased his home in Florida and her stepmom was still in the Caribbean. He sent packages of paperwork for her to sign pertaining to the house. Roberta wondered why she didn't receive anything.

Maybe he was waiting until she arrived, she thought. For now she was just elated that they had their own home. Right now she was even more motivated to be successful as this would be her ticket to get into a doctor of pharmacy program when she immigrated. On completion of that she knew her beloved would not have to be hustling two jobs.

She was now eight months into the program with just four more months to go. The sleepless nights were paying off. She had basically been sleeping for an average of four and a half hours as exams were in progress. She knew she could catch up on sleep afterwards so she told herself to lose sleep now and pass rather than sleep too much, fail, and repeat the entire program. That was a great motivator.

She had received two sets of paperwork pertaining to her immigration. The final set according to Aubyn would arrive anytime now, and she would be heading to her mom's home in St. Elizabeth for Easter holidays. Aunt Lorraine had overheard her talking about it and reassured her that she would FedEx any packages to her as she knew the importance.

Roberta got two weeks for the Easter break and was scheduled to work the week at her friend Eva's. One evening as she got in from work, her mom told her that Aunt Lorraine called to inform her that the package she was expecting had arrived. Roberta had to complete her week at work. Not only did she have to keep her word, she also desperately needed the income. She would work on the papers next week when she was free for the whole week.

Aunt Lorraine, however, did not care for her choices, as Dims informed her.

"Lorraine called again," she said. "In fact, she just came off the phone. She was quite upset. She said to let you know you need to come and take care of your business, and that if you don't care enough to take care of your business that's entirely up to you."

"Mommy, does she realize I went on holiday from school Friday, and the following Monday I was on the job? I hope you explained that I was not twiddling my thumbs."

Roberta was irritated. "What does she expect me to do?" she asked. "I can't just walk off the job, and when I go up there she no doubt will expect her money. Look what she did to you with the partner draw, and now this. She even told me she would FedEx the package, so why the abrupt change?"

Her good friend Arthur traveled as a drug rep between Kingston and St. Elizabeth a couple times per week, so she thought that was a good alternative.

She called her friend and explained.

"Roberta," Arthur said, "I already went to St. Elizabeth for the week, but tell you what. I will be in May Pen tomorrow night, and I can stretch my trip to Mandeville for you. Would that work for you?"

Mandeville was one city down from May Pen, so Roberta was touched that he was willing to drive to Portmore to get her package and leave it in Mandeville for her to pick up.

"Arthur, you are a true friend. I owe you big time for this one. You have no idea how much.

"Anytime, Roberta. Just tell me where in Mandeville you want it to be left."

"I'm sure it will be fine with Maxine. I will ask her to confirm," she told him. She gave him the address to her aunt's house and basic directions.

Sure enough, while she was on her way from work Arthur told her that he had just left the package with her friend in Mandeville. The very next day she picked it up on her way home.

He is truly a great friend, she thought. She still had one week of holiday remaining after she was done working. She didn't have any plans and was simply looking forward to waking up leisurely with nothing pressing to do.

Since she was with her mom and her mom did not have Internet access, she had to use phone cards to communicate with Aubyn. He called her almost daily while she was with her mom, but the calls were understandably curtailed.

The air in the country area where her mom lived was fresh, and emissions from vehicles were almost unnoticeable. She attributed this to the many trees. She remembered she would be returning to the city on Sunday, which was quite a contrast.

She only had four shorts months to wrap up the program and Aubyn's trip to get her was tentatively scheduled the very month she completed it. She arrived on Sunday to find her aunt watering her many plants.

Aunt Lorraine greeted her with a smile. "Come and give your aunty a hug, girl. Do you see how time flies? You just started, and you are almost done! Your friend Arthur is a peach. You should treasure a friend like that. You know like I told you I was planning to FedEx the package to you, but your Uncle Lou advised against it based on the nature of the package."

Roberta did not respond to that because she was sure it would have been safe. It had been sent by mail in the first place. What was important was that she received it, did what was required, and returned it promptly.

The last four months at school were even more stressful. She thought she had lost sleep before, but she soon lost even more. There were at least two presentations a week. She was mainly doing hands-on training now where she had actual patient cases. She had to do several of them per day. This included knowing the case thoroughly and being able to do a pharmaceutical workup on each and sometimes what was called a Subjective Objective Assessment and Plan from a pharmacist's perspective. She had to be prepared because questions could come from any angle. For most cases she was also required to do a formal PowerPoint presentation.

She had just about two months remaining. She was just able to get by when all her savings were consumed with a little relief and holiday jobs she was able to do. Of course, what her mother-in-law had sent her was such a help. Her aunt also only took half the payment for her for the past holiday as she was only there for two weeks. However, she had no choice but to ask her husband for assistance for the final two months of her schooling.

She worried about asking him as she knew he was now paying a mortgage and was already working two jobs. She feared asking him would make him push himself even harder. She carefully added up her expenses, and she only needed the minimum to get by. She decided that if she got US$200 for the next two months she would get by just fine.

She called him as usual then he said, "Are you OK, Sweetie?" He was beginning to learn her ways and could detect subtle changes in her voice.

"Yes, of course, I'm fine. I am excited that I am finishing up in just two more months." Her voice did not sound excited, though.

"And what else 'cause I get the feeling you're not telling me something."

"Aubyn, I know you have a lot going on, and I did not want to ask, but I really tried and I still I really need your help for these last two months," she managed to tell him.

"Sure, hon. Do you think $500 could help you? I could send you that now and then another $500 next month."

"Definitely. In fact, I will do just fine with $200 for the next two months." It meant so much to her because she knew that it was a sacrifice on his part, and she loved him even more.

She needed to dispose of her car before she immigrated, so she told a number of people. So far she had three potential buyers. There was her friend Rhea, Janine, and someone Sammy knew. She had paid to get an evaluation on her car to ensure she was getting the right price and to be fair to any prospective buyer.

Aunt Lorraine offered to purchase it, but said she needed to get her own evaluator as she thought the asking price was too much. The evaluation had a recommended price as well as a "forced" sale price, or the lowest recommended sale price in the event that the owner had a limited time frame. They agreed on the latter, and she sold the car to Aunt Lorraine.

Her final and biggest presentation was due Friday morning. There would be a panel of four professors critiquing, grading, and asking questions at her presentation. In addition, the presenters would have quite a large audience as it was mandatory for the third-years to attend and the second-years were invited.

She had gathered her information, done her research, and thought she was sufficiently prepared for tomorrow. All that remained was to work up the PowerPoint with special effects.

That proved to take much longer than she had thought as she was no professional typist and knew only basic PowerPoint. Aubyn always told her *always* to have a backup other than the hard drive when she prepared documents. "Computers can crash," he would say. "Never forget that, and you have to save your work constantly."

She ended up typing most of the night. She only slept for an hour and intended to get at least another two hours as soon as she was done, but that did not happen. It was already 5 am, and she had to get dressed to leave the house between 5:30 and 5:45. There was just so much to fix and fine tuning to get done.

Suddenly, her computer froze, and then the screen went pitch black. Her laptop had done that before, but it had rebooted afterwards. She panicked, and the tears came streaming down. What was she going to do? There was no time to redo it, and even if there were the document would never be the same.

It was almost three in the morning where Aubyn lived. How could she call him at such an hour? If she didn't get help, however, she could be severely penalized. She entered his pager number on her cell phone and hoped he would not be too upset.

He called her immediately, and she could not hide the trembling in her voice or her crying. He was more worried than upset and sounded exhausted. She felt worse for disturbing his obviously deep sleep.

"OK, dear. I understand, but you have to calm down. Where is your flash drive?"

She did not have one, but she didn't bother to say that. She told him she had only a few minutes to get out of the house and beat the traffic.

He calmly and patiently tried to get her through the steps, and she calmed down enough to follow instructions. Her system was up and running again, but the question was, were her data lost? But no, she saw her work was still there.

She screamed, "Thank you! Thank you. All the pages are there. Thank you, dear. I love you. Gotta run."

"Dear, as a precaution, just email that same data to yourself at least. That's your back up. If the system crashes before I can remotely access it you can retrieve it from someone else's PC."

"I love you, love you," she said as she sounded a kiss for him to hear. "Thanks a million. I really have to go. Talk later."

The day finally came to an end. She thought everyone did so well. No one would even imagine what she had gone through before the presentation, but she was sure others might have shared a similar circumstance.

She was happy when the day ended. She got stuck on two questions, but she felt she managed to receive a good score nonetheless as she answered all the others well. That was officially the last piece of work. They took class pictures and little group pictures here and there.

Roberta thought about her own situation and how different it was. She would be leaving for another life in another country with the one she would be spending the rest of her life with starting the next week. The feeling was bittersweet. She was drained, but that was OK because she could rest up now. She had accomplished what she had set out to.

She went to church with her aunt and uncle that weekend as usual. She no longer had her car, so Uncle Roy picked her up that Sunday, and they were on their way to her mom's home in St. Elizabeth.

She only had one week before Aubyn would come to get her, and there was so much to take care of. Her friends and family came constantly to see her. Some gave her a card or token to take with her, while some cried and made her cry too.

It was truly difficult for her as she had never dreamed she would immigrate. She would miss her mom more than ever, but she had to go join her husband.

CHAPTER 10:
THE REUNION

Sammy drove her to pick up Aubyn at the airport. They embraced for an extended time when they saw each other as if time stood still and they were oblivious to everything else. Normally shy and reserved about displaying affection in public, she discarded all inhibitions. He kissed her on the forehead, and they held hands to Sammy's car.

At least he was staying for a week so she would get a seven more days with her family and friends on her beloved island. She still had things to take care of.

There were personal documents that she wanted to have his name added to, some of which required his signature. She thought as her husband it was only right that he benefit from any of her investments, regardless of how small. She also needed to go into her bank to have the proceeds from her car converted into US currency.

She had received the equivalent of US$3,000 for her seven-year-old car and would be taking $2,200 with her. She was aware she would not be walking straight into a job, and, although this was not much, at least she had something to contribute. She was sure it would come in handy someday for them both.

They confirmed their flight on Sunday and were scheduled to depart Monday October 17, 2005. She knew she would not be able to take many of her things with her, but there were so many personal things she didn't want to leave behind. It was a difficult choice.

There were some books that she treasured that she just was not leaving. She would be returning to school again eventually after she settled in a bit, and she knew some of those books would be good references.

"Oops," she said as she was finishing her packing. "I knew I was missing something, my autobiography." She was one of the few who had received an A for that project, and she thought she deserved it because she did put her all into it. Besides, it held very special memories as she spoke about her life from childhood culminating in her marriage. The theories of Freud and Piaget were brought to life as she highlighted the different stages.

As she looked at the suitcases that were bulging at the sides she wondered how they would be able to lift them. Sammy's car trunk was packed, and since her mom was traveling with them to see them off it was good to see her Uncle Roy turn up. He had said he would be driving his small truck along with Sammy, but she didn't count on it as she recalled past occasions.

They quickly loaded the remaining suitcases into his truck, and they were on their way. From her mom's house it would be at least three hours. The weather was bad, however, and rain had been pouring for days, so they anticipated a longer drive time. Uncle Roy drove behind Sammy, who always wanted to be the leader. She noticed they took an alternative route. Uncle Roy soon caught on and followed suit. They then realized the reason for the sudden change.

It had been raining heavily for days, and they could see some impassable roadway in the direction they would normally travel. They were traveling very slowly, but they had left extra early so there was adequate time. It was the usual 6 pm flight, and they needed to be there at least by four. When they crossed the St. James border she knew they were doing well with time.

They were there before four, and to their surprise the normally packed airport was almost deserted. They checked the monitor, and their question was answered. The non-stop flight on airbus A320 flying Mobay to LAX was cancelled.

"What? But we confirmed yesterday," Aubyn said.

"Let's go to the counter to speak directly with someone," said Roberta

The gentleman at the desk apologized profusely, but said everyone had been notified via email or contacted by telephone. She hadn't checked her email since yesterday afternoon, so that must have been why they did not know.

The gentleman told them they could get a flight out that night, but it would be a connecting flight, and the wait between flights could be as long as five or six hours. The alternative was that they could be placed in a hotel at Air Jamaica's expense and hopefully be on a flight the next day. He could not guarantee that it would be with the same airline, which meant it might not be a non-stop.

While they agreed to the latter, the last thing she wanted to hear was that there was a delay. They were already dressed, luggage packed, and she just wanted to get to their destination. It required so much effort to pack to ensure her things were able to fit, and it bothered her that interfering with anything would result in a tedious task.

There was a waving gallery at The Donald Sangster International Airport where her mom wanted to wait until boarding time so she would be able to see them walk the flight of stairs right into the aircraft.

Roberta didn't get to have a proper good-bye with her mom with all these unexpected changes, and sadness engulfed her. They were beckoned to take the shuttle and at that moment they were scurrying to avoid missing the ride to the hotel.

They arrived at the Jamaica Grande Renaissance Hotel to find that no room had been secured for them. It was the airline's responsibility, however. The receptionist made some calls, and in a short while they were escorted to their room.

It was a gorgeous room, actually, a suite. All other rooms were taken. It was a blessing in disguise. In addition to an elaborate bedroom, they had a large sitting room and a luxurious bathroom complete with a Jacuzzi.

Food was buffet style, and there was a wide assortment of sumptuous food from which to choose. The stay was relaxing and felt like a honeymoon all over again. They ate and leisurely enjoyed the facilities, and then they strolled back to their suite where they spent time enjoying the Jacuzzi.

They were notified by a telephone call in the morning that they would be flying midday and taking two planes. They would be on their way, but changing planes required them to reclaim their luggage, and she feared the suitcases would succumb to the pressure as they were too full.

Aubyn had quite a bit to eat that morning, but Roberta barely ate. She found herself urinating ever so frequently. On the journey to the airport Sammy had to stop twice for her to use the restroom.

Her mother joked, "Hmm, only pregnant women go to restroom that often."

Roberta dismissed the idea as quite unlikely, but she was having slight stomach cramps. She figured it was because she never ate much. The suitcases were heavy, and after they were unloaded from the trolleys it was a struggle for them both. They were constantly required to lift them unto counters at different checkpoints for customs.

Never had she been checked so many times in an airport. The bags were bulky and apparently drew more attention. It was the most difficult thing to have the overly packed luggage rezipped after they were examined by the officers.

Just as she feared, the luggage with the most weight broke. One of the wheels gave way, and the zipper failed. It was hard enough to pull the heavy load and much worse with a defective wheel. As Aubyn stayed in front and pulled the luggage, she tried to secure the contents. After securing two bags, they still had to pull the other two and carry their hand luggage.

Aubyn was getting frustrated. "Roberta, I feel like I am doing most of this by myself, and I can see people looking at me as if they are pitying me as I struggle with all this."

"I have been pushing them toward you to make it easier as you pull. If you're referring to the lifting, I cannot lift them, Aubyn. I know it is a hassle, and I really wish I could make it easier, but I can't lift any of them. I'm doing the best I can, really," she told him.

This should be one of the happiest days of her life, she thought, but it was not. She was beginning to feel like she should not even board the flight.

As it was, they boarded around noon. She hardly ate at breakfast. They changed planes after a two-hour wait. By 3 pm her stomach really felt cramped.

They barely spoke on the flight as disbelief gripped her. She really felt hungry, but the airline didn't take cash and she did not have a credit card. She expected Aubyn to offer so she didn't ask. Luckily she had brought half a dozen cans of Supligen, her favorite milk drink, and quite a few packs of green banana chips. She offered some to him, and he ate.

She had always traveled on her national airline, where she was served one meal and a snack. She had expected the same service. She was surprised and disappointed that everything on this flight was for sale.

When they arrived at the airport they were greeted by Rupert, who was driving Momsy's van. Rupert explained that Dean had driven his car also in order for Aubyn and Roberta to travel more comfortably while the luggage would be placed in the van. Dean, however, had been confused by the new tight security at the airport and left. The step-up in security required everyone to keep moving and to stay clear from the curb unless their passengers were already waiting.

The ride home was still comfortable as it was a big van and the luggage was way out of their reach. It was a ride of conflicting emotions, however, as Roberta felt like turning around and taking the next flight home. Her family and friends would never imagine that she could be having such thoughts, and all she wanted to do was cry and never stop. She hoped this was just an unfortunate event and not a precedent.

When they arrived at his mom's house it was already past midnight.

"Dear, did you want to use the restroom before we go?" Aubyn suggested. "It's only twenty minutes to the house, but while we are here maybe you should."

She felt some compassion for him as he looked worried and seemed sorry for the day's events. She went to the restroom, and it felt like forever. She did not realize how much she wanted to go, but when she did she couldn't stop voiding. It was a tremendous relief after she was done.

They thanked Rupert, and then Aubyn drove Momsy's van to their home. He would return next morning as it was packed with their stuff, especially hers, and it was close to 1 am. Confused and exhausted, they barely spoke for the short ride.

When they arrived at what would be their home, he said, "Home sweet home," as he attempted a smile. She managed to smile back at him.

She already knew it was a nice, older house. She had been to the home twice while his aunt was still living there.

It was already late, and it was a detached garage so they had to get the luggage into the house quickly. They were done in no time.

"You might not want to talk to me, right?" Aubyn said. "I'm sorry about today. I don't always handle pressure too well, and everything was just going so wrong. It was supposed to be a happy day, me coming to get you. Do you know what I mean?"

"Yes," she told him. "It's fine. Don't worry about it. We can talk more in the morning. I really need to get something hot to drink. My stomach still has cramps.

"Oh yes, you poor dear. Here you go. Do what you need to do. I'll get that for you." He hurried to make her some hot chocolate.

"Thanks," she told him.

She wanted to believe that this was just a horrible day, but she was somewhat concerned about the side of him she had seen. Now she wondered how much she really knew this person. She got up the next day and shook off all doubts. She looked around the home, their home, with a sense of pride. He did this for them, and she was proud of the invest-ment. In the back of her mind she did wonder why he didn't choose a different area as he had mentioned to her when he first took her to see his aunt that the area was improving, but not one of the best areas. He told her his mom encouraged him to get it as it would be an investment. Later on they could get another house when she got established.

There was a beautiful home for sale next door to his mother. She had been encouraging him to get it. Roberta was not sure why he did not go along with his mom's first suggestion, but she preferred the choice he made.

In the morning she noticed the back yard was nice and green and well-enclosed. It would be nice and private for an outside meal. She didn't stay outside very long because it was so cold. She wondered if she would acclimate to this kind of weather. He showed her how to operate the heater as he turned the heat on.

He had to return his mom's vehicle, and then someone would drive him back as she did not have a driver's license for the States as yet. She stayed home as she tried to unpack a few things and went into her kitchen to organize things the way she preferred. She noticed he had done some shopping. She decided she would do some baked chicken and potatoes for dinner with vegetable rice. She didn't think he would be staying away for long, but she started anyway.

He was back in a short time. As he entered the kitchen, he said, "Hmm, it smells like someone lives here now, Hon. What are you mak-ing? I could help."

While she was at the sink he rested his head on her back and encircled her waist from behind. "This is feeling good. I am liking this. Once we get you set up in the system here and you start working, we will be good to go."

"Talking about work, when do you go back?" Roberta asked.

"I don't want to think about it, but I return this Sunday night," he answered.

"That's not bad. You still have four days left," she said.

She liked his being at home and was not looking forward to his going off to work, especially since he did the evening shift. He told her that although he had the security system set up, it didn't have monitoring. He would take care of that before he resumed work.

Roberta had not seen her mother-in-law since she came up, but it was only Tuesday, and she was sure she would be seeing her soon. If not, they would stop by. Aubyn had several movies he wanted to watch with her, so they decided they would spend the evening doing that then head to bed.

As an avid musician, he cared about the quality of the sound. Even while watching movies she noticed he had to have Surround Sound as he claimed that it added to the effects. The other thing that she would need to get used to was watching movies in the absolute dark. She was fond of family movies, comedies, and high school movies. He would watch those as well, but was more into mystery, action, and horror.

That night she started watching one with him, and she asked if they could watch it in the daytime instead.

"That's no fun," he said. "Whoever heard of watching horror in the daytime? OK, we'll watch one that you prefer tonight, and I'll just watch this later."

She did not want to be a spoilsport, so she told him she would watch it with him. She really did not enjoy it at all and just knew she might see all that in her dreams. She closed her eyes during certain scenes and told herself that would be the last such one she'd ever watch. She was just dying to sleep when it ended, and though he looked wide awake he decided against watching another and came to bed with her instead.

They would not be getting out of bed early. They planned to enjoy time together in bed.

It was 7:30 am Wednesday when they heard a honking at the front of the house. They did not get up at first, still half asleep and thinking the neighbors had an impatient visitor. She thought that was not polite to be honking the horn at all, let alone repeatedly.

She noticed he looked through the window then pulled on his robe and used the remote control to open the gate. She was puzzled, and as he ran to get the door he said, "It's my mom. Let me go let her in."

Roberta pulled her robe on also and went to wash her face in the bathroom. When she joined them in the kitchen Momsy reached for her and hugged her tight. She seemed oblivious to the fact that she had woken them up. She asked about the flight and welcomed her to her new home and asked how she liked it.

"It's nice. I like it, and the furniture in the sitting room accentuates the entire room," she told her mother-in-law.

"My dear, that is a long story, but I am glad you like it. I went with Aubyn to choose one that we thought you would like, and he said you would like this one."

"I really do like the gold color and the large matching gold stripe cushions. The side tables and lamps create a rich effect," Roberta said.

"There were nicer ones that I saw, and I tried to tell him that he should take another set instead, but he was determined that you would prefer this one, so I am pleased that you do like it."

"By the way, Momsy, would you like a hot drink and some breakfast?"

"Yes. Thanks. I had a rough night at the hospital last night. Ever since I got there at 11 pm I have been running all night, and while I brought food I couldn't even touch it."

Roberta was busy fixing breakfast for everyone while her husband and mother-in-law were talking. She overheard her asking her son, "So how is it going? You think you can manage?"

"Yeah we'll be all right. In fact, tomorrow she has some money she wants to deposit, and I want to help her place her resume online. We'll be fine, Mom. Oh, and the alarm. I'm going to pay extra to have it monitored, especially since I return to work this weekend."

"You can't afford it. I have had my system for years, and I don't have monitoring on it," Momsy said.

"Mom, I can't go to work and leave her like this. I would not be comfortable, and you know what can happen in this area, and if I do overtime I will not be back till morning."

"Nothing will happen to her. She will be fine. Trust me on that," said Momsy.

"Besides, I have my keyboard and other instruments, and I would just feel more secure," Aubyn told her.

"In that case you might be right 'cause if anybody thinks they could steal the instruments they might. Check it out. It might not be that expensive, and if it is I can assist you with that."

Roberta did Johnny cakes and served them warm with the tuna she cooked with tomatoes, garlic, and onions. They ate together, and in no time her mother-in-law said she had to run as she had several things to attend to. She said she got off work at 7 am and had to pass the cross street to their home to get to her house, so it was convenient to stop.

CHAPTER 11:
THE PRECIOUS GIFT

Weeks went by quickly, and she found she had been living in California for a month already. It was already mid-November. She had not been feeling well at all. She felt nauseous every morning, and it had lingered throughout the day for at least a week. For the past two days now she had been vomiting at least once per day.

She used to love having a cup of cold milk, but now it had to be flavored. She could no longer cook beans as she would throw up at the smell of them, and the very sight upset her. She had to stop using perfume.

She was almost sure that she was pregnant. She was excited at the thought and hoped she was indeed expecting, but wasn't sure her husband was ready to hear that news just yet. She decided to tell her mother-in-law in the morning. Momsy stopped by three or four times per week on her way home from work. Roberta was almost sure she would be seeing her in the morning as she had not seen her the previous day.

By now they had gotten used to Momsy's notifying them of her arrival. As Roberta expected, around 7:30 am she heard a horn honk. Lately she touched the horn just once or twice and not quite as loudly.

Her husband reached for the remote that was on his side of the bed as he opened the sliding gate to let her in.

"Hey, Momsy. Come on in," she said. "Here, let me make you a hot drink."

"I am rushing this morning, but I didn't see you guys yesterday so I said to myself I should check on you guys."

Her husband came out greeted her. "Hey, Mom. How was work? OK, I'm going to see if I can get a bit more sleep." He yawned and headed back to the bedroom.

Momsy and she sat down, and Roberta just managed to get her a hot drink before the retching started.

"Yes, this is what I wanted to talk with you about," Roberta said. "This has been going on for over a week now, and the vomiting for at least three days."

"If I may say, I was thinking from the other day that your facial features look different, and I could see it in your eyes that you are expecting," her mother-in-law said with a sparkle in her eyes.

"I don't look any different at all. He hasn't even noticed. At least, I have not said anything and he hasn't either, and I don't think he wants to hear it either."

"Well, he is going to hear it," Momsy said as she dismissed the comment and continued talking. "Like I was saying, I am talking from years of experience, and I am looking from a trained eye. Remember I have been a nurse for over forty years now and spent a great part of that as a midwife."

Roberta made a quick dash to the bathroom, and the vomiting started. Her mother-in-law rushed in behind her.

"You will need to make an appointment today, and he needs to take you in, OK? Where is he? Didn't he even hear all of that? Is he deaf or what?" asked Momsy.

"I don't think he can hear because the door is closed in our bedroom and I'm all the way over here in this bathroom."

"What can you eat then? OK, tell you what. I'm going home, and then I'm going over by Stater's to see what I can find, but you wake him up and make an appointment for today."

Roberta did not want to wake him up, but she would be entering their bedroom to get a shower soon so he probably would anyway. She showered and managed to dress feeling awful and hungry, but unable to eat. The only thing she wanted at that moment was oranges. She had two and did not throw up. She felt she could eat a dozen of them. She finally woke him up and told him his mom suggested they go to the doctor.

They went to his doctor at one of the Kaiser facilities where she filled out paperwork and was given a temporary card. She was impressed at how she was processed as a member and told her card would be mailed to her. The facility was large and clean, and the service was great.

It was their turn to go in to see the doctor and to get the test done. She was so filled with joy, anxiety, and anticipation but scared of the news for her husband's sake. The doctor came out with a wide grin on his face and turned to Aubyn first then to her to say, "Congratulations. You are going to be new parents!"

She was overjoyed, but with a smile quietly told the doctor thanks while her husband said, "Yes, thanks. New parents. That's right."

She wanted to jump and scream but concealed her emotions because, just as she had thought, he did not share her excitement.

The ride home was extremely quiet while she deeply wished he were as happy and excited as she was. He was very somber and quiet instead and looked worried and perhaps even sad. When she got home there were messages on her phone. Her mother-in-law had called repeatedly as she was dying to hear a confirmation. She returned the call immediately, and she could hear her screaming with joy in the background. She only wished her husband could share the same joy.

She still had credit left on her international phone card, so she called her mother right away. Her mother was screaming with joy too. She only had one grandchild, and it was a boy so of course this time she was hoping for a little girl. She wondered who was more excited, her mom or her mother-in-law.

They agreed her name would be Robyn. Both Roberta and her mom had arrived at the name independently about a year ago while they were looking ahead and thinking of girl names. Roberta remembered telling her mom one day as they sat outside of the Fontana pharmacy in Mandeville that she came up with a name. Before she could say anything her mom said "Robyn."

She was so shocked and asked her, "How did you know that was what I was going to say? I never told anyone 'cause it just came to mind this very minute!"

"Well you are Roberta, and he is Aubyn, so the only name I could find off both your names is Robyn," Dims said.

"That's cute and makes a lot of sense, but I did not even think of that. I just out of
nowhere thought of Robyn because it seemed so simple and cute for a little girl," said Roberta.

Like Momsy, her mother wanted to know Aubyn's reaction to the news. She didn't tell her mom the truth. She couldn't tell her mom that he was not excited, but she did level with his mom.

That evening, true to her word, Momsy came over with some chicken lasagna. Surprisingly, she was able to eat large portions and not only enjoyed it but tolerated it.

Aubyn left for work at 2:30 pm on his regular shift but said he would try for overtime and would not be back until morning if he got it. Momsy arrived after 4 pm, and she was happy for the company.

"Don't worry about Aubyn," she said. "He will come around. Everything is new to him: the marriage, the house, and now a little one on the way. I think he was hoping you would get established here first, but don't you worry, I'll talk with him."

She was so grateful to her mother-in-law for the food. Her stomach had not felt full or normal for days. She showered and sat in bed watching a comedy, then ended up flicking from one channel to the next as she tried to find something else that would make her laugh.

If he were coming in he would be there by 11 pm, but it was already past that time. She checked her email, but there was nothing. He did say if there were overtime available he wouldn't be coming in, but still he would usually email her a short message from his pager to let her know. She felt sleepy now anyway, so she turned the television off, went through her quarterly, read the bible verses that accompanied it, said her prayers, and went to bed.

She heard the security gate open before 7 am, so he must have been relieved earlier. She jumped out of bed to meet him at the door. She always met him at the door when he got in from work, especially when he came in late. Since the garage was detached she didn't want him fumbling with any keys. She wanted to let him in quickly.

That was not her reason for meeting him at the door as that time of the morning was not a safety issue, she thought, but she just wanted to greet him. She patiently waited until he parked, gathered his things, and came to the door.

She opened the door with her robe around her and a big smile on her face. The smile was instantly erased as a stone face greeted her. He mumbled a hello under his breath and headed to the bathroom. The depression that enveloped her was so unbearable that tears filled her eyes. The behavior was so unexpected, and what a drastic change it was.

Momsy did not stop by that morning, but she called around 9 am to say she would come see her in the afternoon. There were two plastic bags filled with oranges that Rupert had dropped off for her. She did not have a juicer, but she sat and juiced one entire bag by hand then mixed it, strained it, and placed it into a jug that they both could use when they wanted.

He would be leaving for work again by 2:30 pm so she started dinner early in order for him to eat and then she would pack some for his lunch. She made him a hot dog for breakfast, and he normally had cereal so breakfast was easy. She wanted to do rice and beans along with the vegeballs she was preparing with raw vegetables. She still could not tolerate the scent or the site of the cooked beans, so she steamed white rice instead.

He entered the kitchen, thanked her for breakfast, and sat down to eat. She knew he was going to bed right after he ate.

"Have you seen any job offers in the pharmacy technician field since we placed your resume online?' he asked.

"I have seen availabilities, but one was in Corona and the other in Los Angeles," she answered. "Los Angeles is a quite some distance, and I wasn't sure where Corona is."

"Just keep checking them, and as soon as you are feeling better we have to have you take the driving test. So here, start reading this book for the theory aspect of it."

She took the book. It had questions she could study, and they were quite simple. She knew there would be no problems with her memorizing the information.

"Also I'll be off in two days. We can walk across to the Community Hospital and get you an application and go to a couple places. We have to get cracking, girl. Call me around 1:30 pm, although I'll set the clock as well," he told her.

She finished the dinner and packed his lunch with the lid partially open to allow it to cool before covering fully. She then dished some in a plate for him and covered it in the microwave.

She was about to wake him up when the vomiting started. Some caught the kitchen floor and dripped on the dining room carpet as she ran trying to use her shirt to catch as much as she could. The bulk of it soaked right through her shirt and made its way on the bathroom floor as her stomach repeatedly did the involuntary contractions. She felt like there was absolutely nothing left to come out of her stomach. It felt raw and empty.

The bathroom opened into the master bedroom and he was lying in bed as she hung over the toilet. As soon as she stopped, she grabbed a bucket, poured some bleach, and cleaned the toilet seat. She then got another cloth with fresh water and bleach and cleaned the floors. The last place she had to clean was the carpet. She went outside and got yet more fresh water and another cloth, poured some Pine-sol, and started on the carpet. She then washed the cloth thoroughly and repeated the steps.

All this time he never attempted to assist her and never asked if she were OK. When she went into the room he wasn't there, and she didn't care. She changed her clothing, cleaned herself, and plopped into bed. The sobbing started and felt like it wouldn't end. The only time she heard him again was when he quietly opened the door, peeped in, and told her, "I'm off to work. See you later. I'll be coming home tonight."

She didn't turn around as she answered, "See you later." She must have fallen asleep because she was awakened by the honking of a horn outside. She jumped up and peered through the window. When she saw Momsy's van she quickly opened the gate from inside.

She was so hungry and felt so sick. Her mother-in-law had several shopping bags in her hand. Roberta thought she was probably bringing her more food to try that she might like as she had liked the lasagna. Roberta had been eating lasagna for a week and had craved it up to that point, but she no longer felt for that either.

Momsy had brought her a whole pot of chicken soup with lots of carrots and pumpkin that Rupert specially prepared for her. The soup was a savior. It was the best thing she could get for her hollow stomach, and best of all she liked it and tolerated it.

The nausea and vomiting was almost as certain as day followed night, and she wondered when it would stop. It went on for five long months. She could depend on her mother-in-law at least three days a week to bring her something. Rupert made her chicken soup at least once a week, which he sometimes dropped off but mainly sent with his wife.

One day while Aubyn was on his day off, Roberta had a craving for pastry. She wanted something sweet, which under normal circumstances hardly appealed to her. The pastry shop was less than ten minutes from their home.

"Aubyn," she said. "When you are done playing the keyboard could we just take a quick run across to the pastry shop? I just have this longing for cheesecake or anything similar would be fine."

"I don't feel like going over there now. Maybe my mom will stop by and she could get it for you," he said.

"If I had a driver's license here I would go, and it's just across the street. It won't take you long," she urged.

"I'm always going on the road. Today is my day off, and tomorrow I will have to take you back to the doctor. I feel like I never get to do what I want to," he complained.

The only other thing sweet that she could think of was oranges, and she settled for that.

She thought maybe if he weren't rushing he would get it for her on the way back from the doctor's appointment. Otherwise, she would ask Momsy, and she could drop something off the next day on her way from work.

She had a scheduled visit approximately every six weeks, and this was her third. She did not throw up that morning, but there was nothing in the house she wanted to eat. Aubyn had bought her lots of vanilla flavored soy milk last time they went shopping, and she had been using a carton every two days. This was the only thing she felt for this morning, so she quickly had that and they were on their way.

Dr. Powell had done an ultrasound at the last visit and was unsuccessful in determining the sex of the child. She was hoping for a girl while Aubyn did not express a preference. All that mattered, however, was having a normal, healthy, beautiful baby. The sex was of less importance, she thought.

As they were called into the doctor's office she was so anxious. Her curiosity was at an all-time high as she might find out today.

"How is everyone doing today? Now let's see if the dancing baby will show us what we need to see today," joked Dr. Powell.

The baby was dubbed the "dancing baby" when on the first attempt Dr. Powell had tried repeatedly to see it clearly on the monitor, but the baby kept "dancing."

"Looks like he is doing a samba or meringue or cha cha. Whatever it is we aren't finding out today either. Which one of you is the dancer in the family? He is dancing again, all right," said Dr. Powell.

They were a little disappointed again, but they had a warm, caring doctor, and she was glad she had him. He made everything seem ok.

When she got out of the office she was alarmingly hungry and badly wanted a chicken sandwich. She told her husband, and they pulled over by a McDonald's where he bought her two. She ate one and brought the other with her. She was sure she would feel like having it soon. He bought a hamburger for himself, which he took home.

It was mid-March already, and she was given a tentative due date around end of June. So many things were happening at the same time, but one great relief was that the vomiting stopped. It only occurred if triggered by strong perfumes or the scent of peas or beans cooking, and she already knew to stay away from unflavored dairy milk.

She was not scheduled for another visit until the end of April. As the time drew near, the anxiety did also as well as the fear of childbirth. She had heard so many horror stories about how painful it was. She remembered one of her mother's friends describing labor as feeling like a knife was cutting into her back.

There was so much going on. Aubyn fell in love with some homes in a residential area called Sweden Estates. They had started to build some new homes, and he was set on qualifying for one.

The thing was that he had just purchased the house they currently lived in. They would need to start advertising for a tenant or there would be no way it would be possible. The new homes at Sweden Estates would be completed by June, so there was not much time.

They placed the ad on the Internet in March with an available date for June. They got lots of responses, but many lost interest when they learned of the exact location. Finally one family was interested, but wanted to move in by the beginning of May. Aubyn saw the response and told her, "See, if the new home were ready we would be sure of a tenant now because these people really want it."

"We can let them have it by May," Roberta said.

"How can that happen? That's a whole month early."

"We could stay with your mom for month. I'm sure she won't mind. That way we will secure a tenant rather than wait and risk not having a tenant when we need one."

"You know, I think that's wise. Yes, I'll send them an email now and tell them it will be available for early May then," said Aubyn.

At least that was resolved. He told his mom, and she was elated that they would be there at her place just about twenty minutes away.

It was already April, and she was due for another six-week checkup. She had reminded Aubyn, but she noticed while she was getting dressed he hadn't budged.

"Aubyn, if you don't get out of bed now we will not make it on time for the doctor's appointment."

"I'll ask my mom. I don't think I can make it. I have so much going on," he told her, looking and sounding depressed.

She could not believe it. Today might be the day when they would be able to find out the sex of the baby, and he did not even remember or seem interested.

"It's already after 9:20 am. The appointment is at 11, and you know it takes an hour to get there, and you know how parking can be. Please, call her now. Do you even know if she is home? You know she does not have a cell phone."

He got on the phone and called. Momsy was still in her work clothes and agreed to come over right away. Roberta feared they might miss the appointment because it was still around twenty minutes for her to drive over to their place to get her.

She was happy to hear the impatient horn honking in what appeared to be even less than fifteen minutes. She grabbed her purse and ran out to meet her.

"Aubyn said he wasn't feeling well and he just wanted to rest, and I think it's the nightshift taking a toll on him. It takes a while getting used to it, and he has been doing overtime between two to three times a week," Momsy said.

"Yes, I can imagine. But how come you have been doing the night-shift for all these years?" Roberta asked her mother-in-law.

"Girl, it took a while getting used to, but after I got used to it I love it. It is the best shift. I have all the day time to do what I need to."

Roberta did not agree because losing night rest was not healthy and Momsy hardly even slept in the daytime when she got off. She operated off two to three hours just before going off to work, and Roberta was concerned it would catch up with her.

Her mother-in-law could see Roberta was concerned about the time and told her, "We'll get there on time. Parking will be OK because with my bad hip, remember, I have the handicap parking."

They made it in the nick of time. Dr. Powell asked her for her husband, and she told him he was unable to make it so her mother-in-law brought her instead.

"So are we going to find out who this dancing baby is today?" he asked.

"I think we can wait until the next visit when his dad will be here." It sounded different for her to be referring to him as such. She liked the sound of it and hoped he would too.

Momsy stopped at the grocery store on her way back, as usual telling her daughter-in-law to try different things she might like. Although vomiting was a thing of the past, there were still many foods that she could not tolerate or just had no appetite for. She really appreciated Momsy's doing this for her.

Momsy did not tarry. She saw her get inside and then rushed off saying she had so much to get done. Aubyn opened the door to let her in.

"Oh, it's today they were doing the test? So did he stop dancing enough for us to find out?"

"We didn't do it," she told her husband. "I told him we would wait until you were there, and he says my visits will be every two weeks now."

She hadn't talked to her mom or stepmom in a while, so she decided to call them. She reached for her phone card to call her mom first. She checked the balance on her phone card the way she always did before making international calls. She thought she had $15 remaining when she last used it, and she hadn't used it since. She remembered she had bought a $20 card and only made a short call last time, but now the balance was only $5.

As far as she could tell Aubyn only made calls within the area, and he usually used the house phone. She hardly ever heard him on the phone in the first place, let alone to use her phone card.

"Aubyn, did you make calls with the phone card?" she asked, puzzled.

"Yes, I was talking to a friend I hadn't spoken to in a while," he said.

"This must have been a lengthy call for you to use that much unless you used it more than once. Did you make those calls today?" she asked him.

"Yes, I called today," he said.

"Who is this friend?"

"It's a girl. She has been a pen friend for a while and—"

"People typically write to pen friends, not call them, unless she is more than a pen friend. I had sympathy for you today thinking you were ill or in a low mood, but I guess you weren't." Her voice trembled.

She called her mom and stepmom, and her calls were much briefer than she intended them to be. She was feeling so alone and disappointed and didn't want them to know. The one thing she had longed for all her time in school was to be with him, and she felt like she was having a bad dream. It didn't feel right; something was just not right.

They didn't say much the rest of the night. He felt like a stranger, and she wondered if she really knew him or not. As she lay in bed she flipped through the channels hoping to find something that would make her laugh. She had not laughed in a while. She got lucky and watched *Three's Company* then *The Cosby Show*, and she felt lighter. She read her bible, said her prayers, pulled the covers over her head, and went to sleep.

In the morning he was lying in bed with his laptop, which was how he spent ninety percent of his time while at home. She was nearsighted, and even if she cared to glance she wouldn't be able to see what he was doing next to her. She always wondered, however, what he could be doing online so often that required so much time.

She knew he was always easily worried about finances and figured whatever he was doing was remedy enough to de-stress him. She woke up many times to go to the bathroom, and he would be at it even up to 3 am. She felt guilty that she hadn't started working, and the finances might be stressing him out. She sometimes felt concerned about him that he wasn't getting enough rest, but he tended to get annoyed when she asked, so she stopped.

It was fast approaching the last day of April, and they had to move out of the house by April 30. Each day after she fixed his dinner and packed his lunch she did a little more cleaning and packing. There was so much to get done and very little time. Her stomach was much bigger, her feet were swollen, and her movements were so much slower.

She and her mother-in-law had been picking up a few things here and there for the little one that, according to her obstetrician could be there, in as little as eight weeks. She didn't have a chest of drawers for the little one yet. Ever so often during the day she folded and refolded the few pieces of clothing she already had for the baby. It brought on such intense joy as she tried to imagine the little one in the clothing, her very own baby.

It was already two weeks since the last visit and she had to go in. It was Tuesday, April 25, and after two previous attempts to determine the baby's sex she hoped today would be the day. Aubyn was working that afternoon, but it was a morning appointment, and she was glad he was able to go with her. If he were not present she probably would delay it again like last time. She wanted her husband to be there to share the special moment.

They did the ultrasound, and although the baby was not moving quite as much as he used to, this time the legs were crossed. Dr. Powell patiently waited and kept moving the sensor over her very large, melon-shaped stomach as she felt him put on some more gel. It felt cool on her stomach, and she did not mind waiting if they could find out today.

"Hold a minute. He uncrossed his legs. There is no mistake. Look, it's a boy!" exclaimed Dr. Powell. She was glad the suspense was over, though all that mattered was a normally healthy baby.

Both her mom and mother-in-law had expressed that they wanted a girl. Momsy had no grandkids, but having two boys of her own, she hoped for a granddaughter.

Aubyn smiled at the news and commented, "I'm actually relieved it's a boy. They are easier to raise than a girl, especially with what's going on in this day and age."

Roberta was glad that they had been buying baby clothes in neutral colors. There were some blue ones, but she had definitely avoided pink. Aubyn's aunts and cousins were panning a baby shower. It was not totally a surprise as she knew his family liked to throw parties, and a baby shower was no exception. They told her about it just few days before the shower. It was such a rush as they had two days to get the last of their stuff out of the house before the tenants moved in.

She had done most of the cleaning already. The second bathroom was not used much, so thankfully she did not have much scrubbing to do. It was already after 2 pm, and the shower was set for 4 pm. Aubyn was off today and started to transport some of the furniture with Dean's assistance.

The only cleaning that remained was vacuuming the carpet and cleaning the windows. When they took the last of the stuff out of the house, she would do the final mopping at that time. She was pleased that with proper planning she got so much done. She was still pressed for time, though. She really had to get the vacuuming done that day, and she did.

He was on his third trip to his mom's house transporting everything except their bedroom set, the refrigerator, and some small personal items. She could see he was tired as he had been at it all morning. They would be moving the rest of the things out tomorrow, which was a matter of lifting as they were all packed, and the smaller items Roberta had placed into labeled boxes.

She was ready to go at 3:30, but Aubyn had not yet returned and still needed to get ready. His Aunt Noreen called her and said she would come get her since Aubyn was running late.

The shower was held at his Uncle Guy's and Annette's house just about twenty miles away. She was impressed at the turn out. There were at least two dozen people there. It was fun too as she was blind folded and given gifts and was expected to identify them with little hints.

Aubyn and his brother arrived an hour late, but everyone knew they had little choice. One of his cousins who hadn't seen him in a few months exclaimed, "You look good, Aubyn. Never thought you could gain weight! You even have a 'married man paunch,'" She jokingly touched his stomach.

It was a good day, and Roberta really thanked them. She received several gifts ranging from diapers to monetary gifts. It was interesting that when the gifts were purchased the sex of the baby was unknown, but all the colors were fitting.

April 30 came, and it was with mixed feelings that she lifted up the last few small items that she could manage into the van. This was the first home they had lived in as a married couple. It was their own home, and now they would be sharing space with Momsy, Rupert, and Dean. There was ample space for everyone as it was a large, five-bedroom house. It would only be for a month, and then their dream home in Sweden Estates would be ready.

The homes were moving at an impressive rate, and each week Aubyn and Roberta drove by there to see great improvement. So much paperwork was required. Both Aubyn and his mom seemed to be constantly signing papers. Aubyn told her she was not required to sign on anything yet, as they required proof of income and she was not yet employed.

Both her husband and mother-in-law had a meeting with an agent at Momsy's house, and she was asked to sit in. They were all seated around the dining table for the meeting. Momsy had turned the air conditioner on, but she still complained of being hot.

"Roberta, go and get the standing fan in my bedroom. It's taking a while to cool down in here," said Momsy.

Roberta came back with one she saw as she entered her mother-in-law's room.

She slowly brought the fan over to her, taking twice as long as her feet were so swollen. Momsy smiled and thanked her.

They both discussed the house while Roberta listened and wondered why she was even at the meeting. At the end of the meeting Roberta's legs ached so much she told them she would go lie down in order to elevate them.

Later that evening Momsy came to check on her as she rested in bed. She looked at the top of her feet and said, "This is pitting edema. In all my years as a nurse it's only few times I have ever seen it happen so suddenly. Your feet were normal up to last week."

Roberta had been standing a lot lately, and her doctor had told her she needed to rest more and elevate her feet. It was so puffy and painful, she really needed to.

It was difficult for Roberta to watch Momsy get in from the night-shift and tend to plants. When Momsy eventually got into the kitchen to prepare dinner, it took up so much of her time.

She wanted to see how quickly she could get Momsy out of the kitchen and into bed, but she had such a struggle as Phena spent much of her time answering the phone and making calls.

Roberta had to sit on a stool and rest her legs on a chair to prevent her feet from swelling any more. One evening, Momsy wanted to prepare salmon for dinner, with candied sweet potatoes, steamed rice, and a salad.

Momsy liked fixing the salmon herself, so Roberta assisted by chopping and preparing the raw spices for her. Roberta then gathered the vegetables, washed them thoroughly, and made a very colorful bowl of salad. It looked very attractive and appealing, she thought.

Roberta pulled up a stool as she took care of the dishes. Dinner was all done, and the kitchen was nice and tidy. At least Phena should be able to get ample rest this evening if she did not get stuck on the phone again, Roberta thought.

That evening Momsy was in bed by 5 pm. As she typically awoke at 9:30 she got four and a half hours of sleep, a big improvement from the two hours she had been accustomed to.

Each day Roberta tried to help as much as she could, but as the weeks went by she found she could not assist her with clearing the kitchen like she used to. The longer she stood or sat, the more swollen her legs became. After helping a little she had to head to her room to get her legs elevated.

One morning Momsy was weeding in her flower garden before she even came inside. Roberta and her husband were staying in Aubyn's old room toward the front of the house, so she could hear her outside.

Roberta went out to her and asked, "Momsy, why don't you come on in and have a hot drink before doing all that?"

"You know, girl, once I see the weeds I just have to get it. You know how my days go. If I don't do it now and start something else it may never get done, and you know Rupert's not touching it with a long stick."

Roberta nodded in agreement.

"Roberta, get that machete in the back for me so I can get to these weeds better."

She knew Phena was directing her to the location of the machete, but she wasn't sure what she said and didn't want to ask because Momsy sounded irritated already. She knew it was because the woman was tired.

Roberta looked where she was directed, but did not find it.

"I looked and haven't seen it anywhere," Roberta told her.

"You are not listening. I told you it was..." Roberta tuned her out. It was clear Momsy herself wasn't sure where the machete was.

Luckily, Roberta saw Aubyn as he came in from work and asked him. He found it. She knew Momsy didn't mean to sound mean, but it was coming across that way, and she did not want to be yelled at.

Three weeks passed, and the following week they would be doing another tour of the model that represented their house. Roberta was happy. They got a nice family to rent their first home, and the dream home was at least eighty percent completed. Their baby was on the way, and just the thought of their very own child was too exciting. Their lives were about to change in such a positive way, she thought.

Her husband's face lit up when he spoke about their new home. He was always thrilled at how fast the builders were working. He had not been there in about three days. The last time he went he told her they had done the scaffolding to begin work on the stairway. She had not been there in over a week and was anxious to see the progress. Aubyn asked his mom to accompany them as she hadn't been in quite a while.

The model home was on the way to their house, so they stopped there first. The furnishing and accessories were looked extravagant and truly brought out the beauty of the home so much more.

She knew that her husband had exquisite taste as it relates to home and décor. She herself being more simple had an eye for quality. She still wasn't sure how she wanted their home decorated. Roberta had been perusing many magazines and brochures as she tried to decide. She knew that whenever she saw the right décor it would stand out and there would be no doubt in her mind.

After they were through with touring the inside of the house they took a walk outside to look at the landscaping. The backyard was gorgeous with miniature plants blooming different colors. There was not much earth exposed. Most of the yard was nicely manicured green grass interspersed with a stone work, and Roberta loved it.

"Aubyn, the landscaping is beautiful, I love it. I think we could do our back yard with grass just like this."

"I don't want grass," her mother-in-law blurted out. Roberta was shocked and did not speak for a while. She listened for her husband to comment, but he didn't.

"Why would you say that?" Roberta asked sharply. "Is it because I am not working yet? Now I really don't feel a part of anything. I'm sorry I stated my preference!"

"My mom and I will never forget how you reacted, Roberta. All she was trying to say is that grass is not ideal because it's more to maintain, and you had to get all upset," he reprimanded with his mother looking on.

Roberta was so disappointed. All she was doing was talking about her home to her husband, and now she was being taken to task. All the joy left her, and she turned pale as every ounce of blood seemed to have drained from her face.

They then drove to their new home, which was at the cul de sac just two minutes down the road from the model. Both he and his mom chattered animatedly about the house while she kept quiet. At that moment she just didn't feel like saying anything.

Momsy was overly excited about the house, in Roberta's opinion. They stepped out of the vehicle and walked to the house, and Roberta came out afterwards. There were several boards and construction materials lying around, so she cautiously made her way to avoid a fall.

"Your house is huge, Aubyn. It's much bigger than I thought. You guys will have to have more kids to fill all these rooms," said his mom, smiling and obviously very pleased.

The drive home was too long for Roberta. She was just dying to get to the house to elevate her swollen and aching legs. The visit was not what she expected as she reiterated all that transpired. The good news however was they were told their house would be ready in as little as three weeks.

Her tentative due date was around the last week of June, and so her mom, who had no intention of missing the baby's birth, would be flying in on June 20. She would have liked to fly earlier, but that was the earliest she could get away from her job. That would also be her last day in the work arena as she was also retiring. It was such a busy period; so many things were happening all at the same time.

Roberta was thirty-six weeks pregnant. She enjoyed touching her stomach and feeling her baby move. Occasionally Aubyn touched it also, but he claimed the baby was not responding to his voice like before. She smiled at the thought because he was so sure the baby recognized his voice. She believed he did too, and it touched her heart to hear him say that.

She returned to her normal biweekly visit accompanied by her husband to find that Dr. Powell had started his vacation. He had told them he would be going on vacation, though they had all hoped the baby would arrive prior to his leaving.

They were introduced to Dr. Kane, a tall, pleasant, middle-aged man. He immediately told her she had to stay off her feet as the swelling was too much. He also told them if there were no indications of labor, such as contractions or water breaking, she had to come back by July 11.

When they got home Momsy was there. She was anxious to hear if Roberta needed to go in. She was concerned that the baby didn't seem to have much space to move around. She touched Roberta's stomach and said, "You OK in there, boboo? You don't have much space, eh, boboo?"

The fact that Momsy expressed concern over the baby's outgrowing his space caused Roberta some fear. Momsy kept suggesting that she should go in and her labor induced.

Roberta called the doctor's office with her concerns. They asked her couple questions to which she answered in the negative. They told her both she and the baby would be OK, but to come in right away if anything unusual occurred. Otherwise she was required to come in by July 11.

It was hard to imagine, but the home that they had waited for and watched as it went up was complete. It was June 15 when they moved in. Roberta was overjoyed to be in her own home. She had not forgotten the exchange with Momsy, but that didn't matter right now. This was her home, and she would organize, arrange, and decorate it the way she wanted it.

They moved the first of their belongings as well as that of the baby's into the new home. They didn't hire a truck. Aubyn managed to pack all their stuff into several trips into his mom's older van. That van was surprisingly strong. Roberta cautioned him about using the van to transport the heavy items, such as the refrigerator and bedroom set. That same van had only a month ago transported lots of stuff over to his mom from their other place. She worried that something would go wrong with the van, and that would be an unnecessary expense.

He told his mom that they would be sleeping at their new home starting that night. Momsy was disappointed. "You guys should stay here until after the birth of the baby. What if you need assistance? You guys are at least twenty miles away, and don't forget the hospital is closer from my home."

"Mom, we'll be fine. Stop worrying. We already set everything up, plus my mother-in-law will be here by next week, so we might as well." Aubyn was getting a little impatient.

It was a huge house. It was two levels, with 3,500 square feet and five bedrooms. It felt so huge for only the two of them. When the baby came it would still be only three of them in such a big home. Her husband had always wanted this kind of home. His mom's home was one level. He said he always dreamed of living in Sweden Estates and owning one of those homes someday.

After a week of living at their new home, Roberta found that although the house was huge it was easy to clean and maintain. The main things were dusting and vacuuming. Mopping was also easy for the same reason. The only thing was that her husband had to lift the vacuum cleaner up the stairs when she needed it. Otherwise she managed just fine. She could only do a little at a time due to her advanced state.

She had even managed to prepare two separate meals two days ago that were good for at least a couple more days. She and her husband had no problems with having leftovers, and that made it a lot easier.

Tuesday June 20, brought the day her mom would be arriving. Aubyn wanted the company, and she felt well enough to travel along with him to the airport.

When they got there her mom was already standing outside the terminal. She must have just gotten out because, as usual, he had checked flight explorer before they left and made sure they were on time to get her. Her mother stared at her in disbelief.

"What a way you look big, girl! You were so tiny, now, so big. I hardly recognize you."

"I didn't expect to change so much either. My face and nose ballooned, not to mention my legs," Roberta laughed.

"Anyway, give me a hug. I'm so glad to see you. I didn't expect you to take the trip to the airport. You are really brave," Dims told her daughter.

"Either way, the baby will be here in less than two weeks because if nothing happens I have to go in by the eleventh."

Dims turned to her son-in-law and gave him a tight squeeze. "Hello, Daddy. Are you ready to be a dad?" she joked with him.

He hesitated as if pondering a response. "I am. I am. Just trying to take it all in. Ready or not, here he comes." He grinned at his mother-in-law.

Roberta was exhausted when she got home, and as she expected her legs were terribly swollen, especially her feet. She had not been able to wear any of her shoes in several weeks and had resorted to sandals.

When her mom drove through the neighborhood she exclaimed how much she loved it and that it took her by surprise as no one had given her a hint. When she saw the house she was even more blown away.

"This is beautiful, you guys!" she exclaimed. "I am proud of you. I never would have expected this. It is really nice."

As the days went by her mom could not believe she was not even experiencing any contractions. Roberta, not knowing what to expect from child birth, anticipated the day with much fear. The thought of holding her own precious little one in her arms, however, superseded that fear by far.

She was actually happy when the date stipulated on her chart by her obstetrician came and she was required to go in. With still no sign of imminent labor, it was now clear that labor would be induced.

She opted for an epidural because of all the horror stories she had heard about the pain resurfaced and she didn't think she could endure it. They explained the procedure to her and outlined the apparent risks. She was instructed to stay absolutely still, and it was over in no time.

As she lay on the bed after the induction her vitals were monitored. Her nurse told her she just had two large contractions as displayed on the monitor, but she never felt anything. The nurse explained that she should be thankful for the epidural because such contractions generally did not go unnoticed.

Roberta had been in labor for over thirty-six hours. She had dilated to seven centimeters and could dilate no further. At least now after the induction it would soon be over, she thought, and she would soon be able to hold her precious bundle.

The contractions were coming harder and more frequently, but she still had no idea of the intensity. Her husband, mom, and mother-in-law were admitted into the room with her. The nurse pointed to a button that Roberta should press right away if she needed immediate attention then stepped out for a bit and told her she would be right back.

Momsy was getting anxious. She was concerned that Roberta was still not dilating enough even after the induction. It was clear that she was having difficulty, and the child might be in distress. The nurse returned in less than five minutes and found the baby's heart rate was dropping rapidly. As they all looked at the monitor Momsy could hold her peace no longer, and she yelled at the nurse, "Get the doctor now!"

In no time they came for her and whisked her into a room for an emergency cesarean. Dr. Kane and his anesthesiologist were there, and they prepped her and started the incision. Her doctor spoke with her through most of the procedure. She felt it when they pulled the baby from her abdomen.

There was a huge bawling from the seven-pounds-eleven-ounces as the first gulp of air hit his lungs. A nurse quickly cleaned him off, wrapped him, and handed him to his dad. Aubyn was given the opportunity to cut the umbilical cord. He initially agreed then declined. It was around 2 am Wednesday, July 12, that Robyn arrived, the name so fitly derived from his parents, Roberta and Aubyn.

CHAPTER 12:
SERIOUS PROBLEMS

R obyn must have been extremely hungry. A nurse gave him a two ounce ready-to-feed bottle, and he drank all of it. "He is going to be a big eater like his dad," she thought. After he drank the Similac formula, he slept for so many hours that she was concerned. The nurse explained that it was normal as he had become exhausted due to the prolonged labor as well as exposure to the epidural.

For the next two days he slept much and appeared droopy. She had to wake him up each time to feed him. He barely drank one ounce each time she woke him, which surprised her considering how much he had at his first feeding. Robyn also had difficulty latching on. It was truly an ordeal; she tried so hard, but it was not happening.

Both her mom and Aubyn took turns sleeping at the hospital with Roberta and the baby. One night Aubyn spent the night with them and spent much of the time holding and bonding with his son.

Roberta who, had been resting in bed, desperately tried to get up to go to the bathroom. She was hooked up with a saline drip on a mobile stand so she was able to move. However, as she slowly tried to sit up and pull to the edge of the bed, it was extremely painful. She had wanted to urinate for the past fifteen minutes, but her movements were slow, and each movement reminded her of the incision.

Aubyn was so focused on the child that, although she was struggling for so long and she expressed the need to get to the restroom, it didn't seem like he noticed. The bathroom was located right there in her room, and she managed to get off the bed and was seconds from the toilet when she could hold the urine no longer, and it came rushing down.

All this happened while he was paying attention to Robyn, and it was only when she started sobbing, feeling depressed and not knowing why, that he looked in her direction. She had at least two dozen staples, and trying to sit or stand or lie down was a huge effort. She was accustomed to being independent, and she did not want to be a burden to him.

She had been there for three days already, and she had not yet had a bowel movement. They told her she would not be released until she had one. She was also required to walk from her room down the hallway and back every day to prevent any clot formation, but she dreaded it. Roberta decided she had to start that very same evening as the last thing she wanted was any complications.

"I have been off the job five days already. You better start walking 'cause I can't afford to take off more time," Aubyn told her.

She didn't respond because she had decided that she would start walking today anyway. He sounded upset or frustrated; she wasn't sure which one. She recalled Momsy's telling him he could apply for paternal leave, and he would be entitled to two weeks with pay.

She recalled the conversation very clearly. "I am not applying for that," he told his mom, "because none of them even know I'm married, and I don't need them to know my business."

They had been married for three years, and he had started that job later that same year, yet his marriage was still a secret. He didn't wear his wedding band to work, but he wore it elsewhere. She asked him about it, and his reason was usually the same that the people at work were nosy and didn't need to know his business. She couldn't imagine why, and it did bother her.

Their new home was quite centrally located. It was only fifteen minutes from his job, and many of the stores were close by. The grocery chain they liked shopping at had a store in Sweden Estates just minutes from the house, but he drove fifteen miles to another location to avoid his coworkers. It was the same thing for department stores. There were many close to home, but he would insist that they drive out of the area.

So many thoughts crossed her mind as she tried to figure out a logical reason for his behavior, but none of them made much sense. In spite of it all she was happy for her baby. She would fall asleep, and when she awoke, she still wondered if it were a dream or if she had her own little one.

Each day she hoped she would be found well enough to be discharged as she didn't want to disappoint Aubyn. It was a whole week in the hospital after the C-section that they considered her fit enough for discharge. She was excited to take Robyn home for the very first time.

She hadn't been home for so long, and it felt great being back. Their bedroom was upstairs, and it was not advisable for her to take the stairs for at least six weeks. All her stuff had to be moved downstairs. She had not yet discussed that with her husband.

They had previously bought a twin bed for the downstairs bedroom. It was a blessing. It had a lower mattress that was only a few inches off the floor The other one next to it was much higher.

She was able to sit and pull herself slowly on the lower bed that was going to be hers for at least the next six weeks. She still had a challenge trying to get up from a lying position. It was still so painful. The baby was placed next to her on the bed where she thought it would be easy to attend to him. However, just turning on her side to get to him was very uncomfortable. Her mother offered to assist by taking turns with Aubyn and sleeping on the other bed in the room with her.

Aubyn agreed to spend the first night with her. Once he hit the bed he was sound asleep. She generally didn't fall asleep so quickly. Robyn fussed most of the night. He cried so loudly that she was sure her mom must have heard even though she was upstairs. She tried to comfort the baby just enough to give her time to get slowly to her feet to get his formula. He cried so loudly and wouldn't stop, so it was impossible his dad didn't hear.

When she managed to stand on her feet, she glanced across at him. He was in the same position in which he fell asleep. His face was turned to the wall away from her, and she couldn't tell if he were asleep or not, but she was sure he wasn't. He remained motionless and quiet, and she did not say a word either. She was not going to ask for assistance when it was obvious she needed some.

When she returned to the bedroom with the formula Robyn had fallen asleep. She debated with herself whether to let him continue sleeping or not. She figured he might be hungry so she first checked his diaper, changed him, and fed him. She sat on the bed and burped him, and thankfully he went back to sleep.

She lay down afterwards, but she could not fall asleep. She watched until daybreak, and she didn't think she got an hour of sleep all night. It was morning, and she could hear Aubyn snoring. She got up to use the restroom, glanced at the clock, and saw it was 7:15 am. She felt like a zombie. She knew she had to get some sleep somehow because she felt awful.

Robyn was up when she returned to the bedroom lying on the other bed on top of his dad's chest. At least he wasn't crying. He didn't say anything about last night, and she didn't either.

Aubyn offered to get her a hot drink while she held the baby. Her mom passed by to check on her. "I don't think I slept at all last night," Roberta said. "Did you hear the noise down here from Robyn?"

"No, what happened to him?" her mom asked.

"I guess just being fussy, and he just didn't want to sleep," said Roberta.

"I could keep Robyn tonight so you could get some rest," her mom offered.

She was told she had to drink lots of fluids to simulate lactation. She knew "the breast was the best," according to the popular slogan, and she tried constantly to let him latch on. It was so painful at times as he squeezed her really hard with his gums; at times her nipples got sore.

An electric breast pump would be delivered that same day in order for her to express milk. She was also advised that pumping frequently also stimulated good flow.

The entire day passed, and she never slept as she didn't want to leave Robyn. She only hoped that she would rest better tonight. Her husband said he would sleep with them tonight again, and her mom could for the rest of the week.

She worried that it might be a repeat of the previous night. As usual she ensured his diaper was clean and dry. She was feeding him every three hours, and if he slept beyond feeding time, she would wake him up. Tonight he was still awake when she wanted to rest, so she fed him then, thinking with a full stomach he would fall asleep soon after she burped him.

He did take a while to fall asleep. She sang to him, gently rocking him, but he wouldn't fall asleep. Her mom came and assisted. She stood for over an hour rocking and singing to him before he finally gave in to sleep. She could tell her mom got tired with just trying to put him to sleep.

Roberta lay next to Robyn, hoping to get a good night rest. She slowly drifted off, but woke up. Her maternal instincts were working overtime as she glanced at the clock. She had been only sleeping for two hours when she woke up to check on her son. Aubyn still wasn't in bed yet. She had last seen him on his laptop.

The next time she woke up to what she now thought of as Robyn's trademark as he bellowed at 3 am. Aubyn, who must have just gotten into bed, mumbled, "Let me get some formula while you change him, or did you want to get the formula?"

"Either way, I have to sit up which is still uncomfortable with these staples still in, so whatever you choose to do is OK," she told him.

She went to get the formula while he changed and fed his son. She, however, was left with the task of putting him back to bed while his dad went to sleep. She couldn't wait for the staples to be taken out because she knew then she wouldn't be so dependent. She was thankful that tonight was turning out to be a better night than the previous one.

Weeks went by. The staples were removed, and the baby was latching on. Her mom would be returning home mid-December. Her mom has been extremely helpful and supportive, particularly with the baby. Whenever her mom slept in the room with her and the baby, she was always ready to assist when the baby cried. Without her mom she wondered if she would ever get a chance to sleep.

When Robyn was seven weeks old he woke up an average of three times per night with loud outbursts. She frequently got up with a headache and feeling quite fatigued. She wanted to play it safe, and so she decided to wait until the full two months before attempting the stairs. She hadn't been in her bedroom for that long and wanted to, but decided not to move back into her bedroom until the following week.

Roberta had been sending out applications for clerk and tech positions and to pharmacy school. She researched and found a school that offered a one-year exemption for international pharmacists. Roberta could thus complete the work in as little as three years. It was risky, but she only applied to that one school.

She had already done the TOEFL, PTCB exam and attained very high scores in each. She was selected for an interview for the tech position and had to do a typing test and a knowledge check quiz the very same day. She got an A on the knowledge check, and had two chances for the typing test.

She had never done formal typing and was only self-taught. She was being tested on speed and accuracy and required an A or B, but she got a C. She had the option for the second chance on the same day or to return another day.

Roberta opted to retake the typing test the same day as she didn't want to inconvenience Aubyn a second time. She whispered a word of prayer and tried to focus harder this time. She managed to obtain a B.

It was amazing how quickly she was scheduled for an interview. In only one week she received a call. She felt very confident after the interview and was called the very next day asking how soon she could start. She told them she would be able to in two weeks.

It was already September, and her mom would return home in two and a half months. She would start the job in two weeks. How would she manage with Robyn? She had been expressing milk for him and alternating breast milk with formula, so that wasn't an issue. Momsy worked, and with both she and her husband working, they wondered how they would manage with the baby.

They had heard so many awful stories about babysitters, and they couldn't afford to pay for child care either. When her mom first arrived, she had joked that she was not returning home without the baby. She remembered how she had laughed at how ridiculous that was, but now she was having second thoughts.

That night she discussed it with her husband. "We have to do what we have to do," he told her. She dreaded the day when he would have to be away from her, and she couldn't imagine how she would cope in his absence.

Momsy came by, and Roberta shared Aubyn's and her decision with her. "I am only agreeing because Lorraine must be dying to meet him," her mother-in-law said. Roberta thought to herself the decision was between her and her husband, and they didn't need permission.

Aubyn was dressed for work and had to leave in a few minutes when his mother turned her attention to him. "Aubyn you can't be wearing that to work, the pants and shirt just do not go well together. You are embarrassing me!"

Roberta pretended not to hear. She could not imagine how she would be embarrassed. If anyone should be embarrassed, it should be his wife, and she saw absolutely nothing wrong with his outfit. He was wearing an army green shirt with black pants, and he looked great in them.

As the time approached Roberta got the necessary travel documents, such as the baby's passport and the letter authorizing her mom to travel with the child, notarized. As she put things in place, the reality hit her. She always wanted her baby to be fed breast milk for at least six months, but he would only be four and a half months old by the time he left her.

She received her first study package from the university. It was bulky. There was no guarantee that she would be selected by the school for an interview, but she had to study the entire package in case she was selected. She would not know until April 2007. If she were selected this would be a part of the assessment in addition to an essay and then the interview. Her performance in all three areas would determine if she would be admitted into the program.

It was such a challenge as her shift was unpredictable. She worked days and sometimes evenings, and her shift could change at a moment's notice. She studied every single day between taking care of the baby and her job. She fell asleep over the packet many times, but she had to get through it no matter what.

The day Robyn and her mom were leaving she had to be at work. As a new hire she didn't dare try to get the day off. Their flight was in the evening, so she spent the morning with her son.

She hugged them and told them good-bye. She didn't want her mom to see the tears, but it was inevitable. Now tears were falling from her mom's eyes also. She drove the thirty miles to work, crying all the way. By the time she got there her eyes were red and swollen. Although she wasn't at the airport, she watched the clock closely, and she was mindful of where they should be with each passing hour.

She got home after 10:30 pm, and it seemed like a different house. Her mom had been there close to six months, and now she wasn't there. The worst thing was that Robyn's room boasted an empty crib. This was his home, and he belonged there, but her mom had to return home.

When she went to bed, Aubyn snuggled close, burrowing his head into her chest. She had no interest in being close. The emptiness within felt like it could never be filled. He looked at her and smiled.

"How can you look so pleased when I feel like the world just crumbled?" she asked him.

"I'm not pleased, but what am I going to do? We had no choice, and we know he will be OK. Besides, you have not even had time for me since he came," he answered.

She did not want to hear any of that, and she did not want to respond because her response would not be pleasant.

She rolled away from him, feeling broken, "Good night. I need to get some sleep."

She had asked her mom not to wash the little blue and white stripe shirt that she last saw Robyn in before she left for work. Roberta hugged it close to her, and apparently it provided some comfort as she fell asleep to the lingering scent of her baby.

Roberta bought a $10 international phone card each week just so she could hear how Robyn was doing. Her mom called her almost daily too, and as the days went by she was coping much better.

It was only two weeks after the baby and her mom left that she was to have a major heart break. Roberta and her husband had gone to church that weekend. She came home, prepared a meal, and both ate. He said he was going to lie down so he went upstairs. She stayed downstairs washing the dishes and tidying the kitchen.

The bedroom door was half open; she entered the room, and the position she saw him in deeply bothered her. His laptop was on his nightstand. She didn't care to see what was there, but he appeared nervous and in a hurry to close the screens. Now she was curious and edged closer. She was horrified! Chills rushed down her spine as what he was viewing flashed right in her face.

Roberta was appalled, dumbstruck. *This cannot be happening.* He had so many screens open, and although he tried frantically to close them, he couldn't close them all before she saw.

"How could you do this to me? All this time when I thought you were so upright, so God- fearing, such a gentleman, why?" she screamed at him.

"I … it doesn't mean anything to me, it's an old habit I had years before I met you, and God knows I have tried. I knew some day it would catch up with me."

"I don't want to hear anything from you, not one thing. I wish you weren't here. I wish I never ever had to look at your sick face again!" she screamed.

"I know you don't want to hear anything from me, but I'm going to be honest with you. I need to tell you something now that you know this much," he said quietly.

She stood there, but did not answer.

"I have been viewing these pictures few years now, and I thought when I got married that would help. I also have a friend online for over a year now and—"

She stopped him. "We have been married for three years, so you met your so-called friend after the marriage?" She looked at him and shook her head in utter disbelief. She really did not know this person. All the things that attracted her to him were not real. They were all fake, she thought.

"While the filing was in progress, and you were still out there on the island, this girl and I just started talking as friends. She was lonely, and so was I. You were busy with school, and I really got bored," he said.

She rolled her eyes and looked at him, and crying was now her very sure companion. Had she ever gone an entire month without crying since she came here, she asked herself?

"We talked about everything: the job, the weather. It's only recently we started talking closer and sharing pictures but—"

"So you have been exchanging pictures? What kind of pictures? Have you called her on my house phone, or is it purely the Internet?" she interrupted.

"You should give me credit. You know most men wouldn't even be telling you this," Aubyn interjected.

"You know what? Spare me all this because a true man wouldn't be doing this. So answer me what I asked you!" shouted Roberta. Her head was pounding so hard that she hoped her blood pressure didn't soar.

"I sent her pictures online, and, no, I have not used the house phone to call," he whispered.

"I hope she posts your picture for all to see who you truly are!"

"If you are interested, we will not be communicating anymore," he told her.

"Why should I even believe you? You've been communicating so long, why would you suddenly decide that today?" she asked scathingly.

"She told me she cannot do this anymore because she has a boyfriend now, and it's not fair to him."

"She broke it off because she has respect for her boyfriend, but you had no respect for your wife. How sick is that? Frankly speaking, I wish I never heard this."

She ran to the phone and called his mom. She had to vent, and it had to be now; she had to let it out. It was close to 10 pm. His mom was getting dressed for work, but promised she would be there first thing in the morning.

Momsy was in such a state. She said she felt like she was going to get a stroke and wondered how she would cope at work that night. She overheard him telling his mom that it didn't mean anything, but being online gave him a "thrill." She could not even believe he just said that and truly wondered if he were sane.

Weeks went by, and the way she felt about her husband had changed significantly. For a whole week she couldn't stand the thought of him touching her at all. Ever since they lived together he has been late getting into bed. He would be up many nights until around 2 or 3am whenever he had a day off or even after he came in from the evening shift. He would stay up either watching television, playing music, or working on his computer, but primarily the latter.

Usually when she was ready for bed she would hug and kiss him goodnight, and it didn't bother her, but now she had ample reason to be uneasy when he stayed up that late. At times he would be lying in bed next to her, and she would wake up to use the bathroom and find the space was empty. She was usually right, as he was generally on his laptop.

The tension was so thick in the house. Even though she allowed him to touch her again, it wasn't the same, and their conversations were strained. "I don't know if you'd be interested," he told her "but I think we should get counseling. I am not planning to pay or anything, but there is an online one that is free, or if not, we could speak with our Pastor from Jacinth Ave Church. I'm leaving the choice open to you," said her husband.

"Do what you want to. You tend to anyway. If you want to get the online one, it's up to you or whoever you choose. I'm just tired!" She waved her arms in apparent despair.

The weeks went by, and there was no further attempt at counseling. She felt like they were housemates rather than husband and wife. One evening Roberta went to her bedroom as she normally would, but noticed the door was locked. She banged on the door in disbelief figuring he obviously made a mistake.

"Hold on a bit I'm coming," he told her.

"I'm not going to hold on! Open the door right away; what's going on inside there?" she shouted angrily.

She waited about three minutes, but it felt like an hour. When he finally opened the door, his laptop was on the bed, and he was very solemn.

"This is my room too. Never, ever, lock my bedroom door again. Do you hear me? Never ever do that again," she shouted at him and looked at him with disdain.

Roberta was so angry she was shaking. She didn't even want to look at him. He attempted to explain, but she was crying and shouting so hard that her voice got hoarse. Wasn't it just weeks ago he shocked her with his behavior, and now this? How much more was to unfold?

"I admit I have a problem, and like I told you I'm willing if you want to set up a counseling session. There are several free ones, like I said, but if you prefer Pastor Grant, we could do that."

She thought for a while then wondered if it even made any sense because old habits die hard. She knew deep down she still loved him, though, and strangely enough she felt compassion for him.

"OK, if you think it may help things, then I would prefer to meet with Pastor Grant from Jacinth Ave."

He emailed the pastor that evening, and it was confirmed that starting the following Sunday he could meet with them every Sunday afternoon for two hours at their home.

She heard from her mom almost daily. If Roberta didn't call, she would. Roberta was impressed to learn that after Robyn had been there without them for several weeks he was able to identify his parents' pictures hanging on a wall in his grandma's home. Her mom said she showed him only a few times and ever so often he would point and say, "Mama," or "Dada."

The university had called her at home and also sent her an official invitation for an interview for the doctoral program. She knew there were several applicants, and she considered it an honor to be selected. There was no guarantee that she would obtain a spot in the class, but this was the first step, and she had as good a chance as any. She told her husband, and he was elated. She called her mom and her mother-in-law as well, and they didn't seem surprised.

Pastor Grant was true to his word and turned up the Sunday they all agreed on. His first meeting was mainly introductory. He asked basic questions as he tried to get a feel for the situation then he outlined the approach he would take.

The following Sunday, Roberta hurried through the cleaning and mopping. She was halfway through the cooking when Pastor Grant got there. He asked who wanted to go first, and Roberta volunteered.

After she spoke, he addressed the issues, and then after Aubyn spoke, he addressed those issues accordingly.

Of all the topics discussed, the one thing that she took with her was when the Pastor said, "What he is going through in no way indicates any inadequacy on your part. It shouldn't be taken personally. Rather it's somewhat like a drug addiction he needs help, and that he is seeking."

Hearing those words helped to put things in perspective, especially coming from a professional. It was also promising that Aubyn was the one to suggest counseling, which meant he wanted help and he wanted the marriage.

Several Sundays had passed, and Pastor Grant faithfully met and counseled with them. They have already met with him four times. For this particular meeting, however, he apparently was running late. Aubyn and Roberta were awaiting his arrival at 12:30 pm which was the designated time for the appointment. Aubyn looked at his watch to see it was 1pm and Pastor Grant still had not shown up. Roberta was especially concerned as he was known to be punctual.

They emailed him to find out what had happened. He responded with an apology for not notifying them on time, but explained that he had prior engagements. The following week they too had an obligation and sent him a message to inform him that they were unable to meet. He never responded, and that was the end of the sessions. Although they have seen him at church on a regular basis, he never mentioned the subject and neither did they. There were definitely fruits from the sessions, but they were abruptly discontinued and everything was left hanging.

It was the month of May, five months since Robyn had left. It had been such an eventful period for her that she coped with the baby's leaving much better than she anticipated. She had received the call from the university in April, and her interview was scheduled for the third week of May.

She had gone over the packets at least twice and planned to go through a third time quickly, so she felt prepared. Robyn and her mom would return on Tuesday, May 15. She was so anxious to see her baby. He would be nine months old when he returned, almost a year. Her mom had a number of things of her own to attend to, but she hadn't expected him to be away for longer than three months. Her mom didn't really use the Internet, and the one picture she had seen of Robyn since he left was one her brother had taken when he came by to see their mom.

It was such a strange feeling, seeing her baby again. He looked so different in the picture, and she felt almost like a stranger to him. Roberta had planned to sit in the back in order to ride home next to Robyn. Both she and her husband offered her mom the front seat, and as she settled in Robyn started climbing over and reaching for his grandma.

It almost broke her heart that the chubby little baby didn't know she was supposed to be the closet person in the world to him. She caught herself and thought about all this time it had been he and his grandma, and it would be a while before he understood. Her mom told him to sit with Mommy while Roberta tried to guide him back to her, and he cried, still reaching for his grandma. All this time his dad sat there observing the happenings.

"Robyn, show me Mommy," his grandma said. She was astonished when he pointed and touched Roberta. "Robyn, show me Daddy." He pointed and touched his dad on the head.

That was definitely reassuring, Roberta thought. She just wanted things to work out somehow so that there would be no need for this back-and-forth business. The following week was her interview. She was done with the packets and now focused on asking herself some possible interview questions.

Things were looking better for them which she attributed to the meetings with the pastor. She even noticed that Aubyn no longer kept the laptop in their bedroom. Her mom still did not know what had transpired between them. Roberta thought that was for the best, knowing her mom would have her say regardless of who got hurt.

Aubyn called his wife, acting all stern like an interviewer, and she had to laugh in spite of herself. It had been months since she had laughed like that, and it felt great.

"In fifteen minutes meet us in the formal living room for your interview." He tried to look serious and professional in formal clothes.

Roberta was all ready for her "interview." She arrived earlier than required to find her mom and husband straight-faced holding notepads and pen. She also noticed that a video camera was mounted and ready to start rolling. She wanted to tell the "interviewers" that recording the interviewee without her consent was illegal, but she didn't bother. She was going to do her very best as if it were the real thing to boost her confidence even more.

They both assumed different names for their roles, and Roberta laughed at the introductions. Of course, the "interviewers" weren't laughing, so she played along with being very serious too. "I am Dr. Goodman," Aubyn said, "and to my left is Dr. Erickson. We have some questions for you today. Our aim is to learn more about you. At the conclusion of the interview you will also have an opportunity to ask questions in return."

She was asked about ten questions in total. Her husband had been through several interviews himself, so he had little trouble compiling pertinent questions. Her mom did a great job as well most likely due to her teaching background.

Roberta had done her own individual preparation: but it was no comparison to the mock interview they had carefully orchestrated. At the end of it, of course, when the camera stopped rolling, she thanked them. She gave her husband a big kiss and hugged her mom tightly.

She wondered how long they had been planning this because not a word had she heard from them. It was well organized, so she imagined it had been planned long before the "interview" day.

CHAPTER 13:
FURTHER STUDIES

The day for the real interview came, and she was not too nervous. He drove her down to the campus and left. There were so many prospective students and that wasn't all because it was a two-day interview.

They were called in to take the written test, which included multiple-choice and an essay question. Her previous university commonly used essays as a mode of testing, so she was comfortable with that. She felt confident so far, but waiting to be called in for the interview stirred up a little anxiety.

When it was finally her turn, the atmosphere was more relaxed than she expected. She felt at ease with the interviewers. It was amazing that the questions were quite similar to what she had been practicing. She was asked five questions, and although worded differently they were all typically the same. It would not be a month before she learned her fate. That was going to be a long wait. She had to find a distraction so she wouldn't dwell on it.

As the weeks slowly went by she kept counting down; the third week of June seemed like such a long stretch. Every day as she attended to Robyn and did her routine chores, it was never far from her mind. She repeatedly questioned herself. *Did I do well enough to be selected or not?*

It was so much more difficult to be one of those selected because all were qualified. Roberta was applying for the international pharmacist program. All candidates were already registered pharmacist with a minimum qualification of a bachelor's degree that they had obtained in another country, usually their country of origin.

Many prospective candidates had received study packets, but only 120 were selected for the interview. Of those interviewed, only twenty with the highest possible score would be chosen. It was a three-year post-grad program, as the twenty successful candidates would join the second-year class.

Gilford and her stepmom called her generally a few times every week. They must have grown tired of her constantly fretting over whether she got accepted or were sympathetic toward her. She was offered a ten-day trip to their place in Florida. She was grateful for the break.

Roberta and Robyn took the trip there, and the change of environment made a difference. Even though she still wondered about the outcome of the interview, she did it less than while at her home.

The week she was scheduled to leave Florida was the same week she should be hearing from the university. She called every day to see if there were any word for her. It was so coincidental that the day she was in transit awaiting her flight to return to California she called home and was told that mail arrived from the school.

Aubyn told her that Dims was ecstatic and had ripped the letter open. He read her the words, "We are pleased to inform you, Mrs. Roberta Sullivan, that you were awarded a spot into our accelerated international doctor of pharmacy program, congratulations."

She didn't hear anything else that the letter said. She wanted to scream, but the location wasn't conducive to that. He proceeded to read the different areas that she scored the most in and the areas that were a little lower. The specifics did not matter now. All that mattered was that she was so much closer to working in her field here and would be able to assist her husband.

She wanted to shout for joy, but had to contain herself as her setting was so public. She still had at least twenty minutes prior to boarding the airplane, so she called her dad and stepmom. They were elated, and her dad, as ironic as ever, said, "So, Miss Roberta, you didn't choose to get the good news here. You had to get it at the airport."

She smiled. She couldn't wait to get home.

As was expected the entire crew came to meet her at the airport: her husband, her mom, and her mother-in-law. It was one of the best periods and most promising moments she has had in such a very long time. It was a welcome difference.

"You did so well, Sweetie. I'm so proud of you; we all are. It feels like we can really start cracking now. I feel like we are on a path that we should have been on a long time ago," said Aubyn.

"I am just relieved the suspense is over and all that studying was not in vain. I would not want to have to go through that again if I had to reapply," she told her husband.

Both Dims and Momsy allowed Roberta and her husband to talk undisturbed while they chattered together at the back of the van.

"I am taking you out to a celebration dinner. Pick the restaurant, and consider it done," Aubyn told her.

There were at least two she had in mind. She liked Thai food, but she also liked West Indian cuisine and longed for that type of food. She settled on the latter without much hesitation.

Roberta's life was one of continuous activity, and now with the acceptance letter it was going to be a grand rush. Orientation started mid-July, which meant she had just about three weeks to get things in place for school.

School started with a bang. The orientation was short, but teachers also did some review from the first year's curriculum to familiarize them with what their soon-to-be classmates did last semester. The class consisted of only the twenty students. They would not meet the class that they would be merging with for another month. It was quite a diverse group. There were two people from the Caribbean including herself; one third of the group was from India, and others were from Thailand, Vietnam, and New Zealand.

The month passed, and she was beginning to feel what it would be like to be in this program. It was going to be a rigorous course of study. It was a large class since the class they merged with was already over eighty students.

Six weeks after the group merged, they got their first assessment. It was so much material as each lecturer laid it on. The assignments came, and then the quizzes came, and gradually the presentations came. Roberta needed to accomplish 1,500 internship hours before she completed the program. She worked at a community chain as an intern ten hours each week. She not only accomplished her hours, but also was receiving a paycheck fortnightly.

Roberta found it tedious to drive one hour each day to school amidst traffic then onto her job. They came to depend on her little paycheck for groceries. Time was scarce, and she had to juggle between full-time school, her job, and chores. She constantly felt guilty that she never seemed to have quality time with Robyn.

It was a tremendous blessing that her mom was there. Otherwise it would have been virtually impossible. Robyn was already a year old and was an active little bundle. She longed to be able to hold him and not be concerned about time.

Aubyn worked the evening shifts, but at least twice per week he did overtime and would not get home till morning. All she could think of was she had to pass all the exams so that her husband could slow down, and she could be there more for Robyn.

Roberta also received a stipend every six months and religiously split the amount equally. She gave him half of it to assist with their daily living expenses, and from her half she took care of the baby's needs as well as her personal needs. Her husband always saw to the maintenance of the car and paid for fuel.

Once her mom was there Roberta was not worried about cooking, but no matter what, Roberta did the cleaning. Her mom was helping her enough already. The 3,500 square feet was a lot to clean, but was well maintained so did not require too much scrubbing.

The entire year, Roberta studied by herself. She had at least three close friends in addition to groups that she was assigned to for different projects, but she felt compelled to head home as soon as she could.

The year went by, and she did not get as many As as she had hoped for, but at least she passed all the courses. She got mainly Bs and one C. She worked hard, and sometimes during test periods only operated off two to three hours of sleep. She was a bit disappointed, but she made it nonetheless.

It was really true that the hardest thing was to begin, and before she knew it, it would be history. It was August 2008, and she was already in the third year of pharmacy school. If she thought school was hectic, it was about to increase. There were many more PowerPoint presentations and many more quizzes. Roberta was feeling a lot more stressed. She was always tired, and she was missing her baby. Her mom had to return home after being with her for five months, and so Robyn went with her. She wouldn't be seeing her son for at least three months.

It was that feeling all over again as she now accepted that until she was through with school she would encounter this kind of separation from Robyn. She was even more determined to accomplish her goal as more than anything else she longed for the stability of her family. She longed to have a normal life with her husband and child without the constant separation.

The year 2008 turned out to be another interesting year. Momsy came to visit them at their home in Sweden Estates as she normally did. She didn't stay for long that day as she said there was an open house just three houses up the street from their home. She returned in two hours with shocking news.

"I just bought the house up the street from your house," she told them.

Her son shook his head.

"Mom, you are almost retired. What about your other house? What were you thinking?"

"I wanted to be close by so I can help with Robyn so Dims don't have to be back and forth like this," Momsy said.

Roberta listened in utter disbelief. She knew her mother-in-law was not retiring soon, and she was always busy and usually exhausted. How she planned to help with Robyn was really a question she wanted answered.

In just four short weeks after Momsy announced the purchase, she started to move in. She had so many things she said it would take her a year to get everything moved over. Knowing Momsy, Roberta did not doubt that at all.

Now that she practically lived across the street, just three houses up on the other side, she visited frequently. Roberta liked when she visited because when her mom and Robyn weren't there it was only Aubyn and herself. Many times, however, Roberta had to be rushing off to get some work done. Momsy generally left shortly if her son weren't available.

Roberta was up around 8 am one Sunday morning getting the laundry done. The doorbell rang. Roberta had just gone upstairs for a second to get the rest of the clothing. She hurried down the stairs quickly and dropped the clothes and rushed to see who was there. It was Momsy. She appeared very impatient as she continually rang the bell. Roberta rushed to disarm the alarm.

She opened the door with a smile on her face which immediately dissipated at Momsy's countenance. "Do you know how long I'm out here ringing this bell? You have me out here waiting so long," she yelled at Roberta.

Roberta tried to explain that she was doing the laundry, and she was rushing to put the stuff down to get the door. At this point Roberta was hurt and didn't feel like saying much to her at all.

"Where is Aubyn?" asked her mother-in-law

"He's sleeping. He just got in this morning," she told her.

"Poor thing, he is working so hard, I can't wait for the time that he doesn't have to be stressing like this," said Momsy.

Roberta excused herself to check on the washer. She came back to find Momsy standing by the sliding glass door in the kitchen. "I like Aubyn's backyard. I think his backyard is bigger than my own."

Roberta didn't answer; she didn't want to hear any more. "I'm going to rush back to the washing as I have to hurry 'because I have a test tomorrow."

"That's OK. I was leaving any way. Tell Aubyn that I stopped by. Please close the door behind me, Roberta," her mother-in-law smiled at her, obviously sorry for the outburst, but she did not apologize.

She pondered, *Momsy was addressing me, her son's wife. It's my house too. She generally talks as though it's only Aubyn's home and not mine.* That night Roberta went to bed after midnight, preparing for her test. The phone rang close to 1 am. Momsy was at work and wanted to ask her son a question and apparently called without considering that Roberta should already be asleep.

Roberta jumped up with a sharp headache. She could not go back to sleep until around 5 am and had to be up by 6 am to be on her way to school. She went blank on many of the questions on her test as her head pounded. She spoke to her husband about it, but he didn't see it as a big deal. She only hoped she passed the test.

The results were posted within a week after the test. It was convenient to access the school portal to check her results. She managed a C and was happy for it. The rest of her third year was intense, but that came as no surprise. The professors had laid out clearly at the introduction of each module all the objectives. She used those objectives as she studied, and they served as a great guideline.

Roberta took a moment to reminisce. They had both learnt so much from Pastor Grant. She thought even if the sessions hadn't abruptly stopped they probably would be anyway as she was severely pressed for time. She recalled it was quite disturbing when she was informed that it could be years for some habits to change. She was required to be more patient and not to see herself as a failure, but to support him through the "addiction."

She saw some positive changes. He said "sorry" more often, although many times she ignored the apologies, labeling them as excuses. He helped more in the kitchen, chopping the spices, preparing the vegetables, and doing the dishes, although she wished he would keep her company until she was all done. Most importantly, he removed the laptop from the bedroom and placed it in the office. That to her meant more than most things as that was one of his biggest struggles.

It was a Friday, midterms had ended, she would be off for two days, in addition to the weekend. They both were lying in bed. Neither wanted to get up. It was going up to 10 am when Roberta, still with rollers in her hair, felt like doing something different for dinner, something creative. The weekend was coming, and coincidentally he was on his day off as well. It felt great just unwinding and doing family stuff.

"Aubyn, I am trying to make something interesting for dinner, but I am missing the coconut milk and bread crumbs. When you get out of bed, could you please just run to the store dear, *please*?"

"You could go get it too, dear. I just don't feel like running on the road today. I feel like I am always running around. I never get a day to just stay in."

"Aubyn, just please go. I hardly ever ask this of you, but I just this minute thought of it, and with the rollers in and all that…"

"Just go get it, Roberta. I mean, you don't have to even do anything special today. Whatever is fine by me."

Her spirits were instantly dampened. "That's OK. I will just get it myself." She did not speak with him for the next hour until the phone rang.

"Here, it's for you. Your mom wants to speak with you," she told him.

"Ok, Mom. I'll get it then. It's not going to be right away though. Give me about forty-five minutes," she overheard.

Roberta noticed he got out of bed went to the bathroom then returned to their bedroom fully dressed. "I'm trying to kill two birds with one stone," he told his wife. "What was it you said you needed? I'll get it for you since I'm running to Stater's to get a few things for my mom."

Roberta said nothing for a while. She thought she imagined that he just told her no, then not fully thirty minutes later his mom called, and he told her yes.

"No, you don't have to get anything for me. I'll get it. I have no one else to ask, while your mom has her other son and husband who lives there."

"You don't know my mom's situation. She just couldn't go, so I'm going for her," he snapped.

"I guess you know my situation, what I was preparing was for us, but that's OK. I will never, ever, forget that you did this, you hear me? Never! This is just one of the many things you have done."

He went and was back in a flash. He brought everything she had asked him initially. It hurt so badly just because they usually shopped every three weeks. Whatever they needed on a weekly basis either he or she would get on their way home. It was rare that they were both there, and she required this of him.

"Did you want me to help you to make the dinner you wanted? Or if you want, just give me the ingredients, and I will fix it," he said.

"I don't feel like it anymore. It's up to you if you feel like fixing something. I'll just make something else later."

She had so long awaited the perfect weekend just to relax with no need to study as she would be starting the last semester of the third year.

She never expected things to be this sour, and she felt pure dismay. She wondered when or if there would ever be a day when she could just be happy like some of her other married friends. She thought of Irene, who had been married to Barry six years before her. They were still so in love like newlyweds.

The next semester came and went like it didn't happen. January 2009 the class learned about their rotations and was instructed as to how to select their sites. Rotations would begin promptly the following month.

She hoped she got sites close to home as all the previous years she has been travelling a total of one hundred miles per day. Each rotation was six weeks long. Some were compulsory, while others were electives, although they had to rotate through a total of at least eight sites. At this point, she only needed to select rotations for the first few months and she chose a community pharmacy, the County Hospital, and the VA.

She generally went to her job Tuesdays, Wednesdays, and Thursdays. It was not easy to get out on time as there tended to be something last-minute. Her hours at the job were now 8 am to 12 pm three days a week, and she needed to get to her rotation by 1:30 pm.

Robyn and her mom returned right after her final exams as planned so that she could give him most of her attention. Her husband and she were on speaking terms, and although she loved him, she had stopped telling him so, and so did he. Emotionally Roberta was tired, and her spirit felt so quenched. She had one extra thing to deal with, and now Aubyn started complaining that she spent all her time with Robyn and had little time for him.

What did he really expect her to do? Her child was back and forth at least every five months, away from her on average for three months. Most of the time when the baby was with her, she had to be in her books or at school or at her job as an intern. In addition to that, she had not been feeling close to him like she should amidst all the things that had happened.

It was December 2009. Roberta had just started her final year and Robyn was almost three and a half years old. He and her mom were doing the usual trek to the Caribbean. It was still vivid in her mind how her baby had kicked and screamed as he and his grandma went through the security checkpoints at the airport.

It was so painful to watch as Robyn folded his little wrists, beckoning to his parents to come when he noticed they would not be going along with him and his grandma. It was heartbreaking to watch as he became so uncooperative, and her poor mom had a trying time with him. He loved his grandma dearly, but he was older now and had great attachment to his parents in spite of the frequent separations.

Both Aubyn and she were glad that soon enough she would be done with school, and they wouldn't have to go through this ever again. The previous times he traveled, Robyn seemed to be unaware of what was truly happening, so there were no tantrums. Luckily, as he was becoming aware, there would soon be no further need for this.

The very same evening Robyn arrived on the island and saw his two cousins, he was just fine her, mom told her on the phone. As the weeks went by, however, her mom told her he started to fuss about his mommy and daddy.

Now Momsy accompanied them to the airport to pick up Robyn and Dims. The flight was delayed, and there were so many hiccups that by the time they arrived home it was close to one o'clock in the morning. They did not get to bed until around 3 am. Everyone was exhausted.

The next day no one was up until around midday. Robyn had gotten up for food and a diaper change and gone back to sleep, obviously still exhausted. Roberta noticed the flashing light on the phone down stairs indicating there was a missed call. She realized it was her mother-in-law, so she returned the call.

"Why you don't answer the darn phone? You know how long I have been trying to call? I called until I was so mad. Dean wants to use Aubyn's lawn mower, and he could not even get it. I'm so mad." She ranted and raved.

Roberta could not believe this was for real.

"You need to stop right now!" she said. "You cannot call our home and think it's OK to talk to me like this. I certainly could not do that at your home!"

"You know what, Roberta? I am through talking to you. I will get back to you later. Put Aubyn on the phone!" Momsy demanded.

"You have said it all. I really don't think there is any things else to talk about. Here is your son." She gave the phone to him.

As her husband took the phone from her he grumbled loud enough for her to hear, "You caused the whole thing, Roberta, because if you hadn't turned off the phone in our bedroom, I would have heard when she called."

To hear him say that hurt like crazy, but it did not surprise her as he was always defending his mother. She was always wrong, and his mom was always right in his eyes. It should have been a happy day as both her mom and child just returned the day before, and yet here was another big drama. *Never a dull moment*, she thought. It was such a surprise that her own mom listened and never said a word, but if she knew her well, it was not likely she would let it pass.

Roberta decided that there needed to be a meeting. Everything seemed to be totally out of control and simply had to stop. She called her dad and stepmom in Florida. They agreed to come over, and her mom was totally for it too. After many days, Roberta had the courage to speak with her mother-in-law to inform her of what was decided. Momsy was also in agreement.

In just two short weeks her parents arrived, and all six were present with her dad as the moderator. All had their chance to speak. It was done very informally, although ironically they all gathered in the formal sitting room. It was an amicable discussion, even though there were some touchy issues causing some emotional moments. It was a success, and they all emerged from the meeting embracing each other. Aubyn and Roberta decided they would communicate with each other more openly and would invite a third party into daily issues only if it were completely unresolvable between them. As Aubyn put it, Roberta needed to desist from calling her parents as if they were 911 when minor things occurred. There was only eight months remaining in her final year. There were still a few more rotation sites to do, the final project and presentation, graduation to attend, and then the two board exams to take. There was still quite a journey ahead.

Each rotation was unique in some way and involved quite a bit of work as several cases had to be assessed and analyzed. It was purely clinically, but it was a welcome change from the classroom setting.

Roberta wanted to be done with school and finally start working full time. She believed things might be less tense between her and Aubyn, and he probably would be less stressed. There was just so much to look forward to, and it definitely was not far off, she thought as she sighed. For now things were amicable again, and she only hoped it would last.

CHAPTER 14:
PROBLEMS GREW WORSE

Roberta generally went to her job for few hours before going to her current rotation. She was quite fortunate as her supervisor was flexible. She was told as long as she fulfilled her eight hours per day she could either come in on the morning or afternoon shift.

Roberta got off from her job early. She had enough time to swing by her home before heading off to the site. Aubyn wouldn't be leaving for work until 2:10 pm to start the afternoon shift at 2:30 pm, so she would definitely see him when she got home.

Roberta arrived in the garage at their Sweden Estates home as the clock said 12:20 pm, which meant she had at least a half-hour to spare before heading out once more.

When she arrived, she heard Aubyn's voice although she couldn't hear what he was saying. She didn't see or hear either her mom or Robyn. She figured they went for a walk up by Momsy, as they did at times. The house phone was not engaged so she figured he must be on his cell phone. She entered their bedroom. He was not in there, but his cell phone was.

Roberta froze. She stormed into the music room and realized there was a second line in their house of which she was unaware. He practically paled like a ghost when he saw her.

"What are you doing home so soon, dear?" he asked. "What happened? Aren't you supposed to be at your rotation? Your mom and Robyn went by my mom's, so when I heard the door I thought they had returned."

"So we have another line in the house, in my house, and I didn't know of it? Who could it be you're speaking to that you had to get a secret line? Tell me who?"

He still had the other person on the line, and then as if he suddenly remembered, he told the person he would call back in a little bit.

Roberta showed him the handset from the telephone. "Why couldn't you use this telephone? Why? You must have something going on that I'm not supposed to know about."

"Roberta, it's my friend Allison from work. She is just coming out of a difficult breakup with her boyfriend—"

"And I suppose you're the counselor, right? What great concern that you had to get a special line just to call her. How many more times am I to go through your mess? I want to divorce you! My stomach feels upset when I see you. You are sick!"

Roberta threw the telephone down in such a rage that the top broke. She was never known to throw things, but he did lead her to it. The phone was only the second thing she had ever thrown in a rage.

Roberta did not want to go to her rotation, but she had to. She left crying, and her heart felt like it was breaking.

That evening Roberta got in from her rotation after 9:30 pm. Aubyn was not yet home from work as was expected. He would be home around 11 pm. Robyn was asleep , but her mom was up concerned about all the stress her daughter was going through.

"You might have to get out of this, Roberta. This guy repeatedly does things to hurt you, and so far counseling seemed to have failed. You need to start looking out for yourself and Robyn right now."

"I can't just up and go, but, believe me, when the writing is on the wall, I will know then that it's time to go."

Roberta had a lethargic shower and went to bed. She heard when her husband came into the bedroom.

"Hello, Roberta."

"Hi," she answered, and that would be the extent of the conversation if she had anything to do with it.

After he came out of the shower he said, "I suppose you don't even want to see me."

Without another word she jumped up and started throwing all her stuff out of her dressing table. "I'm moving into another room. Yes, I don't want to see you."

The following night she was in the kitchen downstairs when he came in. He barely had time to say hello to her. If he only apologized, she would have accepted it and moved back into the master bedroom.

"Hi, Roberta," he said as he rushed to the house phone saying he was going to call Allison to check on her because they were giving her a hard time at work and the situation at home had escalated.

She thought, *He was at work all evening, I was on my rotation, and I have not seen him all day. He just left work, and all he can think of in the midst of their own crisis is her wellbeing.*

At this point she agreed with her mom and dad that the situation was going to take a serious toll on her health and she should get out. Her stepmom, on the other hand, was suggesting that they make another attempt and get another counselor.

She did not say a word, just went to sleep in the other room. This trend of his concern continued for quite some time. After a week she returned to her bedroom, but many nights he called his "friend'" when he got in and spent over an hour on the phone.

Roberta poured out her heart to him in an email and then in a hand-written letter, but he did not respond. She told her parents about it, and they were livid. She told his mom also. After she spoke with Phena, she no longer noticed his making the calls, but she was sure he was anyway.

Roberta was in and out of the bedroom. She slept in their bedroom sometimes, and other times she slept in another room. Lately she noticed he was getting more calls from his second job. He used to get these calls perhaps once per week or every two weeks, but lately he was getting them at least twice per week.

She did not mind these calls as it meant more income for the family except he would leave home early on these calls. He would travel to the LA area and would often arrive home quite late. At times he didn't even return on time to start his primary job. It bothered her that he might be jeopardizing his main job.

Roberta was relieved when the rotations were all done. She learned a great deal from each one of them, although some of the supervisors sent her home with lengthy projects that kept her up until early morning. Everyone was busy making plans for graduation, and excitement was everywhere. Rotations ended the third week of April, and graduation was scheduled for Thursday, May 20.

She had all four weeks to unwind and just wanted to relax and take care of whatever she had been forced to neglect for so long. She was planning to sit both board exams just days apart in August, so she was planning to study intensely right after graduation.

A few of her friends from the Caribbean expressed interest in attending the ceremony, but at least two of them were unable due to their work situations. Her friend, Sophie, however, confirmed that she would be flying up and so did her brother. Her other brother Andrew also requested time off from his assignment out of country to attend.

She would be hosting a total of nine people, including her immediate family at their home. Momsy had graciously offered to host some of the guests in the event that it became necessary.

Roberta's school had planned a complementary graduation dinner for the graduates that promised to be a special event. The dinner for the graduates and their spouses or other companion was being catered. She was dying to tell Aubyn about it. It was scheduled in Pasadena the evening before the graduation day.

He never failed to disappoint her with his negative responses. He complained that the timing of the dinner was inconvenient and it was too much driving. Her brother had volunteered to accompany her, but Roberta declined. She had been hoping the evening would be spent with her husband.

She could never get a chance to move on from the things that haunted their relationship since he gave her reasons to doubt so many times. She couldn't help thinking about the fact that he never wore his wedding ring to work and never wanted to shop with her anywhere in the vicinity of work.

The proud day of her graduation came when she went up to accept her doctorate of pharmacy degree. She was accompanied on stage by both Aubyn and her older brother.

It was a feeling of great achievement and accomplishment.

She had one other event planned to which she was really looking forward. It took quite some convincing Aubyn to give her the green light. She had met several friends during the course of her rotation from different nationalities. Roberta wanted to have at least seven ethnicities represented, and all were required to fix a native dish. Her brother Everett would be the designated chairperson for the cultural cuisine night she was planning. He had chaired a number of events before and had a natural talent.

The cultural cuisine started promptly at 1 pm. There were representatives from Jamaica, Indonesia, Belize, and Egypt. One of her friends from Africa had to work that day. The others from Vietnam and India had other post-grad events that were totally understandable. Four nationalities were represented, and nothing appeared amiss. It was an afternoon to remember. A total of twenty-one guests fit quite easily in their spacious family room.

When Aubyn had not joined them after thirty minutes, she found herself making excuses for him. In answer to their questions she told them he wasn't feeling well and would come downstairs as soon as he could.

The door bell rang around 1:35 pm, and it was her mother-in-law. Roberta greeted her jokingly with a "Better late than never. The wanderer has arrived."

Momsy, ever the sociable type who chatted feely with everyone whether she knew them or not, furrowed her brows when she noticed her son was missing.

"Where is he?"

Roberta whispered in response, "He is still upstairs. I'm not sure. He just hasn't come down, and he knows everyone is here."

"He makes me so mad! I'm going up there right now to bring him down," stated Momsy sharply.

She knew he would come down now, but she hoped it would not send waves through the gathering.

There were several games and a talent show as well as a raffle. The raffle was drawn by her younger brother, and the lucky person, the Belizean representative, received a gift card.

Her mother-in-law was in time for the raffle, but Aubyn came down about ten minutes later. He had a natural knack with people if he chose to use it, just like his mom. Everything appeared normal. All apparently accepted that he was now well enough to join them. Roberta was glad he turned up even though he came when all the activities were over, but at least he was able to meet her friends and enjoy the food.

It was amazing. The graduation had come and gone; friends and family had come and returned home. She got to spend quality time with Robyn, and it was a good thing because now she had to dedicate the next several weeks leading up to the board exams to study. She scheduled both exams just five days apart, one late in July, the other the first week of August. It was already June. If she started now, she would have at least two months.

There was so much material to cover. In order to accomplish everything she made a time table to which she diligently adhered. She was studying at her desk in the office, and he was at his desk just across from her. She heard him sigh, so she asked what was wrong.

"I used to be able to buy my mom stuff. Now I can't even buy her anything. It's just bills all the time."

"How strange that you would say that. What about being worried about not being able to buy your wife anything?" she asked.

She just turned back to her studies, disappointed as usual. It were as if she didn't matter. When would she really realize that?

"When you start working fully, I really need to save. If only I could even catch up for a year or two. I have been carrying the weight all this time and—"

"As usual I suppose I was never contributing, right?"

"It's eating away at me. I feel like I can't save. This is not what I had in mind. I feel like there is so much to aspire to, and I am just not getting there."

She didn't want to talk about this. She hadn't even taken the boards yet, and he had all these demands already. She looked at him and didn't answer immediately.

"All I'm asking is that you take care of the bigger portion of the mortgage," he said. "And we can split the groceries and utilities since you will be earning more than I do."

"I am studying right now, I really don't think this is the time for that, and you know me, that I am more than fair. I will do what I need to do. I've always been like that," answered Roberta.

Roberta got up from the desk because she had to take a break. She just could not assimilate any more of the material. Her emotions were whirling, and she wanted to scream hard until she could finally have peace and happiness.

She had sent out some applications, and it was so exciting when she received a telephone call in June scheduling her for an interview. The interview went better than she ever imagined. She was hired on the spot. She couldn't wait to share the news with her husband in spite of everything. Maybe now, hopefully, he would be more positive.

She did the first board exams, and the results were in the mail within three weeks. She was nervous to open it. She picked up the mail and walked all the way upstairs before she opened it.

It was good news. She didn't jump; she didn't scream. She just said, "Thank you, Lord."

She was awaiting just one more result and was even more worried about the second exam as the choices were extremely close. By the following week, the results arrived. Aubyn had picked it up at the mail box, and Roberta was just a little hesitant to open it. Her mom volunteered to do it.

"Mommy, I was just going up to my room to open it—" she started as she heard her mom read the word *Congratulations*.

Things started looking up. She had passed both exams in a single shot, and she had a job awaiting her.

She knew she would have to wait at least a good month before she would receive her professional license. The very next day she called her new boss Dr. Buchanan to let him know she was successful in the boards. He congratulated her and asked her when she wanted to start. It was already midweek so she told him she would like to start the following Monday if that were fine with him.

He was OK with her response and said he would forward an email to her outlining her pay scale and benefits package. She would start out fulltime on a graduate intern salary until they received her license. The first two weeks would be training to ensure she became comfortable with the company's system. She would be expected to be fully functional on her own afterwards.

The package looked attractive. She called her husband immediately to read the email. He smiled as he read it.

"Finally looks like things are coming together. By the way, remember to pick a spot, and dinner is my treat any day of your choice," he told her, looking happy.

All that time she had put into her studies, the emotional turmoil of not always having her baby around, and the struggles seemed to have paid off. She had not seen her husband really smile in forever, and she was smiling too.

It was August 2, 2010, when she started her first day on her job as a registered pharmacist. It was training for the first two weeks, both reading modules and hands-on, but she was being paid and she was enjoying it. The practice was quite similar to her role as a pharmacist in the Caribbean. The only difference was she was certified to administer several vaccines, and she liked that.

As the months went by, Roberta felt like she and her husband were working together better as a couple. She agreed to take care of the greater percentage of the mortgage, and they split all the other bills. Roberta was a careful spender. She shopped wisely by comparing prices and always ensured that her family ate healthily.

Roberta had volunteered to assist at a nearby animal shelter. She was not always able to give of her time, but she gave a small gift whenever she could. The first time she sent a check from their joint account, he didn't talk about it so she figured it was OK. She hadn't visited the shelter in weeks so she decided to visit one afternoon after church. Robyn, now four years old, was also listed as a volunteer. There were so many dogs of different breeds and sizes in cages. Her heart was touched. Robyn loved his own dog, Chelsea, that he generally referred to as "my dog Chelsea." She was really his dad's dog. She wasn't able to play like she used to as she was at least 14 years old, moved slowly, and was slightly deaf. When they went for walks Chelsea would stop very frequently, taking long rests. Roberta usually took a water bottle with her on their walks. Robyn had taken the water bottle from her on multiple occasions and offered Chelsea a drink, saying, "Poor Chelsea wants water. Wait, let her drink."

She remembered thinking, *There goes my water.*

There weren't many volunteers, and they walked as many dogs as they could with Roberta taking two at a time and Robyn running behind. The dogs were so excited to get out that they were literally pulling her. She had to hold their leashes quite firmly to avoid their running away without her.

They managed to walk about eight of them, but it was exhausting as she had to be fair to each of them and at least give them twenty minutes of freedom. There was an enclosed grass area about 20 feet from the cages, and as it let them free to roam, they frolicked and dug and rolled.

They had already been there for two hours, and they never got to see the cats. They quickly went to the cattery, petted and played with them, and then were on their way. As they were leaving she saw a sign listing some of the needs. The need was so great, Roberta decided to give another donation. It was only $60, but she knew it would help, and she planned to drop off some canned food for the animals the following week after church.

She had been on the job for seven weeks. It was going great, and she was quite comfortable with the system and thought she had actually found her niche. It was a Wednesday afternoon, just four days after writing the second check, when she got home early, and he was on a day off. She was generally tired at the end of the day as her job required her to stand for the entire shift.

"Roberta, we have to hold unto what we've got," he said, quite annoyed. "We can't be constantly plucking out money and writing checks like this. Who is giving us anything? Who?"

"I gave it to the shelter, and it this was only the second time. I probably will not be doing this for at least another few months anyway," she responded.

"You shouldn't be doing this for another several years," he told her. "Not until we catch up. I suggested a budget; you have not responded. I have my version drafted. I asked you for yours so that we can agree on one together, but you have showed no interest."

"What are you talking about?" she asked. "I paid the higher portion of the mortgage and split all other bills with you, plus I was the one that paid the auto insurance for both vehicles, and we still have a decent savings. So tell me exactly what budget you are talking about."

"I also noticed that you wrote a check to someone last month for their birthday, but if you noticed I said nothing. Seriously if this is going to continue, we will have a big problem."

"The check was for my niece. It's only once a year. What do you want me to do? I really can't take this bondage. I just can't," said Roberta.

"All I'm saying, dear, is that we have to be careful, or we will never have our dream and just keep running ourselves into the ground," explained her husband apologetically.

"Aubyn, I spend wisely. I split the bills. I save. In fact, I have been managing my finances very well on my own before marriage, so why do you suppose I can't do it now?"

"I would say more, but knowing you, you will take it out of context," he told her.

"And what would that be?"

"I don't want you to think I am pushing you or anything, but you have a lucrative job. You could apply for a part-time position elsewhere and earn more for your family," said her husband.

"Do you even care that I have a job where I stand all day?"

"Well, many people do that for their family. I've seen that even on my job, and what about when I was busting my butt while you were in school?"

"You know what? There is no point arguing with you. I guess you forgot how much help my stipend was to you then."

Although the discussion was not a pleasant one, Roberta didn't want to waste energy to show any malice as much as it hurt.

It was Roberta, Aubyn, and Robyn living together as her mom had returned home. Roberta was still thinking that she would ask her mom to visit periodically to assist with the baby. She hadn't yet discussed that with her husband, but at some point she would. He was now in pre-kindergarten, and Aubyn was still trying to get a better shift at his job. It was more likely that he would than she would as she was a new hire.

The month of October was as cold as her relationship. It was exactly five years since she had immigrated, and amazingly seven years and three months since they said, "I do."

Well, she said "I do," and he said, "Double yes."

It was unbelievable how she had been through so much, and now school was a thing of the past. She had graduated and had a job since August. It brought joy to her that she was able to assist her husband in a more significant way. She didn't like to see him working double shifts so frequently. At least now, she thought, he probably did not have to do it if he didn't feel like it.

She was OK with his working overtime once a week, but sometime he seemed so tired. He could choose not to work as hard with both of them employed on a fulltime basis. Lately, however, he had been talking to her about wanting to launch into business with Thein, who had a big venture coming up. He explained to her that it wasn't yet off the ground, but it was bound to succeed as they had everything lined up.

"That sounds good, Aubyn," she said. "But until you see the feasibility just use it as a backup. Remember, your main job is what has been sustaining the family."

"Thein wants me to be available three days per week, so I have already requested to work two days at my state job and—"

"How could you make such a decision and not discuss it with me first? What about our health insurance? How could you do this?" she asked in pure disbelief. "I noticed you worked only two days last week, but I figured your days off had changed again. I just do not understand this. Honestly, what were you thinking?"

"I have to do what I have to do! All this time I have been pulling the weight, and I never got to do exactly what I wanted to do. Now the opportunity is here, and I am taking it!" he yelled.

"I'm not trying to dissuade you from your 'dream,' but you can't just give up your days at your job like that."

She looked at him for a response.

"Go on. I'm listening," he said

"I had no idea you were making yourself available in case Thein had a project for you," said Roberta. "You took those days off permanently from work, and he didn't even call last week, and so what happens this week? This is crazy, and I didn't think you could be this crazy!"

"You don't know the man. He has been in business several years. He has been working on this for years now. There are several investors just waiting to come on board. For heaven's sake we could retire early! The man is taking technology to a new level!"

"I have every confidence that this will work, but all I'm saying you can't voluntarily give up your days when there is no guarantee that he will call you those days, and he has not called. That's a big loss right there, can't you see?" she questioned.

"So what do you suppose I should do? Better yet, you see your man trying to work on something and where is the encouragement? What can you do to help? Why don't you ask yourself that? I wish I had your options. I would be doing a second job easily. You guys are in demand, and you are in a lucrative field!"

Seriously, she could not believe he said that. What more was he expecting her to do? She was already working her full forty hours a week, standing for her entire shift, and still had to be a mother and a wife when she got home.

Occasionally she was asked to do a double, and she did when she could, which meant even more standing plus she drove approximately fifty minutes one way to work. Where was his consideration for her? Was there any love or care left for her? She couldn't help wondering, and she was afraid she didn't want to know the answer.

"I think you should request to be back on your job fulltime, and when Thein is fully on with guaranteed days and benefits outlined, you could request to be part time again," she answered.

"I noticed you didn't care to answer the question about what can you do to help after I have been practically killing myself before you came fully on board," said Aubyn.

"You very well know I have been helping in a great way all this time. You know that. If you are talking about a second job, no, I'm sorry. I have to care about me since no one else does. I am not going to work an extra job when I already am doing my full forty, and you voluntarily gave up yours. It's not happening," she answered angrily.

The weeks went by, and there was no change. She periodically checked their joint account to ensure the bills would be covered as well as to get her direct deposit set up to ensure a percentage went to their savings every pay period. She also had opened an account for Robyn and religiously saved for him each month.

She watched as his biweekly paycheck was slashed in half, and although he received random calls from Thein, she did not see any additional checks. He had voluntarily reduced his hours for close to a month now and complained ever so often that the savings was not where it should be. She had an uncomfortable feeling that he was not being transparent with her.

He constantly pressured her about doing more hours or doing a second job while his job was only fifteen minutes away from home.

He was adamant about his new venture and would have no discussions about it. It was so painful to watch him make critical decisions that directly affected her and Robyn while being totally excluded. She had to fix this, and since only his mom could get through to him, she decided she'd tell her about it. His mom agreed to meet with both of them at her house that very afternoon.

The meeting started out nice and calm until it was Aubyn's time to speak. His mom asked him to explain this new "venture" with Thein. When he proceeded to get Thein on the phone, everything exploded.

Aubyn dialed Thein's number and gave his mom the phone taking her totally off guard and obviously the other party as well. Momsy started to explain to Thein about the disruption that this was causing in the family. The conversation continued until she started to let him know how bothered Roberta was about the stand her husband had taken.

Roberta listened for awhile and was not in agreement as to how the situation was being conveyed. Neither did she see the need for Thein to be involved in this discussion. Roberta started to voice her own concerns in the meeting when her mother-in-law got really upset.

Roberta did not like to be spoken to like a child, and that was just the way Momsy came across to her. Pointing and wagging her finger at her, she shouted, "And you, Roberta, you don't listen. I'm here trying to pacify the problem, and you there are acting up. Who do you think you are?"

"If you are going to talk to me like this, I am not going to listen. I am going to get up and leave right now," responded Roberta.

"Mom, that's how she is. She thinks she is on a pedestal and some princess. Look how you sat me down and spoke to me, and I took it, but, no, she is above that," Aubyn told his mom.

He then turned to Roberta. "Who do you think you are? Tell me."

She was cut to the core. She would never have asked him that question. He was the man she married, and it didn't matter if there were many more handsome or wealthier men. To her he was her "prince," but it was obvious she was not his princess.

Roberta looked at him so humiliated that he would openly side with his mom against her.

Roberta was already standing and ready to go through the door when he said to her, "If that's how you're going to be, you might as well go. This is making no sense."

She knew he meant go for good, and if she had any doubts his mother confirmed it. "Yes, you guys might as well go your separate ways 'cause you are not getting along."

Roberta now knew her fate was sealed. If Aubyn hadn't been thinking that way before, he would be now. As Roberta left the house she felt alone. She truly was thinking that if she had any family member close by, she would move out that very night.

Robyn was somewhere upstairs with his uncle and luckily didn't hear the argument. This was the second time they were having a meeting with his mom, and it had turned out really bad. The first one was an unexpected meeting while they were coming from church and her husband decided to stop by his mom's.

Just days before the unexpected stop Aubyn and Roberta had a quarrel. She had asked him a simple question about whether he were wearing a jacket with his outfit to a family event. He did not answer the question, but rather asked her why she had to ask that and what did it matter what he chose to wear. She felt so hurt and upset. Without thinking, she hurled the hanger that he had laid on the bed at him, and it struck his lip.

She had no idea that he lodged a complaint to his mother and brother about the incident or that his lip was bruised until they stopped at the house. She thought it was a regular visit until Dean approached her to threaten that if he ever heard of any such thing with his brother he would be calling three numbers. She could only guess what those numbers were. They obviously did not know the entire story and probably didn't care to. Roberta just walked right out.

That night after the meeting with Roberta, Aubyn, and his mom, she did not want to go back to their home. The meeting was abruptly ended around 4 pm. Roberta took Robyn, and they stopped by a girlfriend's not very far away for the next several hours. She needed to get away; she needed to vent. It wasn't until after midnight that she returned to their house, wishing she didn't have to. She wished she could get away for good.

CHAPTER 15:
THE DIVORCE WAS FILED

Roberta pulled into the garage after midnight. She had never stayed out by herself that late before. He never even called her to show concern, and her cell phone was on all the time.

"Did you even wonder what you put me and my family through when you left and we didn't know where you went? Did you even consider that?" he asked her.

"I have nothing to say to you. Funny how everything is all about how you or your family feels. I was never in the equation. I never mattered. Don't worry. You'll soon no longer need to worry about me, and then you all can be happy."

"I'm making some hot drink before I go up. Would you like a cup?" he asked

"You can if you feel like it," she answered.

It suddenly dawned on her that whenever he used the phrase "my family" it never included her or Robyn. It was usually his mom and brother. She felt like she was a stranger or even an intruder. She went up the stairs, grabbed her clothes, and went for a long shower.

He came in, announced, "Here is your hot chocolate," and made a hasty exit as though it were forbidden for him to be in the bedroom while she was taking a shower. It looked like it was over, and with tears in her eyes she admitted to herself that although she loved him there was none for her in return. She wasn't sure when it had gone away, but it was definitely gone.

The situation grew uglier each day. Normally he would wake up in the mornings, take care of things he had planned to do. Otherwise he would sit at his desk by his computer or simply lie in bed, but that changed. Lately as soon as he awoke he announced that he was going by his mom's. He stayed there all day until it was time to get dressed for work.

She wondered how Robyn was coping not seeing his dad like he used to. He had been asking her why his dad was staying out so long. It got so bad that when she cooked, she noticed Aubyn didn't eat. Her heart felt so full, she couldn't help asking him why he wasn't eating dinner there anymore. He responded that his mom cooked him dinner.

It was a Wednesday, and Roberta was off all day. He got up as usual and told her he had to take his mom somewhere. He left around 8:30 am. Roberta noticed his van was still parked by his mom's up to around 10 am. She knew she had to get out of this because it was pure emotional pain to watch the happenings around her.

The evening came and turned into night, and he still did not come home. Roberta decided she would not sleep in the bedroom, since the past few nights whether she did or not it didn't matter. Roberta could not sleep, no matter what he generally came back by at least 9 pm. It wasn't until around 1 am that she heard him come in. She came out to see him and asked him why he was doing this when he knew that other than their child she was at home by herself. She was more astonished to hear that he only came to grab something and was heading back to his mom's house.

Lately she no longer knew when he had days off or not as the communication was even more limited. He had gone back to work full time complements of his mom, but this time it was on the nightshift as his mom had always wanted. According to Aubyn she told him that it was less stressful working the nightshift and that there was a better salary. There was no regard for the fact that he had a family to come home to.

It was not getting any better. Roberta called her mom and asked if she could return earlier as things were not going well between them. Her mom arrived three weeks later.

Not much had changed when her mom returned except he was getting home between 9 and 10 pm, and on the days he worked he had to be out by 10:30 pm. It was unusual for him to get home after 4 pm one evening, but he did. She was happy for Robyn's sake as he was pining for his dad. Father and son played video games, then he took Robyn to the backyard, and he rode his bike. It was refreshing seeing her baby happy as he reveled in his dad's attention and laughed so hard.

That same evening he came in and told her he was going into the Jacuzzi and wanted to know if she would join him. She declined. There was so much to talk about, so much has gone wrong, and yet apparently she should just be ready to gratify him. She thought to herself, *I can't.*

She had hoped her refusal would prompt him to initiate a discussion, but it didn't. When he came in some mornings, he was out again without any sleep when Thein called. He seemed to be travelling to LA at least three times per week, and she wondered how he functioned with no sleep. The next several weeks it was the same with all these extra calls from the second job with Thein with no reimbursement that she knew of.

He was always the one to complain about spending, and yet he was often driving these long distances, and there was no check to show for it. She seriously suspected that he might be allowing her to spend money on their family maintenance while he stashed away these extra checks.

Roberta had received cash value for a policy she had in the Caribbean for over ten years. She decided that she would open a separate account with this amount and try to save a small portion monthly for herself. She decided against telling him about it.

She gradually rerouted her direct deposits to this new account.

"I thought you got paid every two weeks, Roberta," he remarked one day. "But I haven't seen anything for you in maybe three weeks."

"I switched banks. I will write you a check for the mortgage and everything else but since you want to be separate, then we will do just that," Roberta told him.

"Oh, so that was the plan. I'm no fool. I knew as soon as you got into your field this would happen. Don't you worry. I will soon fix you!" he threatened.

"Not before I fix you," she told him.

She tried to keep her voice down, but he was yelling, and although she tried to tone him down, he wouldn't. Unfortunately Robyn heard much of it and started crying.

Dims came out and said, "You guys notice I haven't said a word, but now you have gotten the baby into your squabble, so now it involves me."

She turned to her daughter and said, "I don't know why you don't leave this caveman who does not know how to treat a woman. There are so many good men out there. He is not your last chance!"

"Mommy, please, I'll handle it because it's only going to get worse, and now Robyn is hearing everything."

"You should have thought of that before you start answering the caveman," snarled her mother.

"I am getting out of here. In fact I'm moving out, and you can take this house!" shouted Aubyn.

"You know very well the house is not paid off. Are you planning to assist me with the payments considering your son lives here?" she asked.

"No, I will not," was his dry answer.

The very next day Roberta went house hunting. She met with a realtor in search of a house for lease within the same vicinity as Sweden Estates. She didn't want to take Robyn away from everything that was familiar to him, and she still wanted him to be able to see his dad. She was in no position to purchase a house at this time, but she needed to lease a home right away. She hoped that within another year she would be able to save enough for the deposit on a home for her and Robyn.

She was lucky to find a three-bedroom house just ten minutes down the street from the other house. The thought of looking for a house and leaving the home she knew was unbearable. She was still not sure if she wanted to do this. There were several other people interested in the property, and they had to go through all the applications and run credit reports, so she would not know if she were successful for another week.

After the big outburst, there was such calm in the house. He kept mainly to himself. Her mother and her husband had not exchanged a single word since. She had gone back to her bedroom. It was rather inconvenient to get dressed elsewhere when all her things were still in their bedroom.

January 2011 had already come, but there was nothing new about the year. It was the same old pain. There hadn't been any further outbursts, but they only spoke when absolutely necessary. She came in from work, ate, showered, and she lay on her side of the bed with him on his side.

One evening around 7 pm she heard the doorbell ring. She wasn't expecting anyone.

She asked him if he heard the doorbell, and he answered, "It's for you."

She walked down the stairs not knowing what to expect.

She peeked outside and saw his brother standing there. She opened the door and managed a weak smile. He handed her an envelope, and said words to her that pierced her like a knife: "This is a summons from the family court."

As she looked at the envelope she knew what it was. She grabbed it from him, thanked him in a sarcastic tone then slammed the door shut.

He pushed the door open, explaining, "I brought it myself because I thought it would be easier for you to receive it from a family member rather than a stranger."

"Family? Did you really say family? None of you are related to me, none of you!" shouted Roberta.

"I have nothing to do with this, Roberta. All I am doing is delivering this. I hope you know that," Dean tried to explain.

"It does not matter. It's just a matter of time, and this misery will be over. So all those many days and nights he has been at your mom's this was what you all conspired to do. You are all such a perfect match; you all belong together."

She went back in the bedroom where he was and looked at him in utter disbelief. She shook her head. "You are dangerous! You were lying right next to me, and with no warning this is what you did. How cold and callous! To think all this time I thought I knew you."

Roberta went into another room sat on the floor just staring into the ceiling as if seeking for answers. She felt claustrophobic, powerless, trapped. Robyn's and her world just crashed. She could do nothing.

As she sat there the words of a sermon preached by a pastor from The Hill View church seemed to flood her very soul. She reflected on his words, "marriage can be the most fulfilling relationship yet the most fragile. We don't fall out of love with our kids, we don't tell them I don't love you anymore but it's ok to tell our spouses. The very sacred institution that God himself ordained."

She felt like an organ was ripped right out of her, they would no longer be a unit, they would be separate. The divorce begins the finality for them. She permitted herself to continue to recall the words of the sermon. Four key ingredients were essential for a healthy marriage: time, love, communication and prayer and she knew they lacked most. There was no suitable adjective to explain her grief and her aching soul.

The next day she contacted the agent and proceeded with the lease agreement for the property. She was required to pay $3,000, which was the first month's lease and the security deposit.

Whenever she was on the afternoon shift, she ran around in the mornings and got the utilities for the new premises placed in her name.

It was difficult for her. Some of the utility companies required a lease agreement prior to processing the request for service. She reflected over all the years she and her husband were owners. Now suddenly she was starting all over. The sadness took over. The next task was trying to explain this to her four-year-old.

She had called her dad and stepmom in Florida, and they immediately booked their flights. She had not been expecting them to come, but her stepmom was adamant that they had to be there for her.

The agent called and informed her that she was selected over the other applicants for the property. Roberta went and finalized the paperwork and did the payment. She had to be strong for her child. She couldn't allow him to see her crying or looking sad.

Each day she packed a little more of her stuff into boxes with her mom's help. The house would be ready to move into within a week, but she set a tentative moving date for end of January. She tried to make it seemed like fun while she packed, and her son tried to help.

"Why are you putting my books into boxes, Mommy?" asked Robyn.

"Actually, Robyn, did you want to come with Mommy for a ride? I have something to show you."

She had planned to show him later that week, but she thought she might as well do it today since he asked.

"Sure, I want to come. Is it a surprise?" he asked, beaming all over.

"Yes, you can say that, and I hope you'll like it too," replied his mommy.

"Yippee, but I want to help first!" said Robyn as he grabbed arbitrary things and dropped them in the box. She knew she had to redo the whole thing, but right now he was helping, and that made him happy.

They drove for ten minutes down the road and pulled up at the house.

"Why are we stopping at this house, Mommy?"

She tried to explain that this would be his other house as both of them will be there along with grandma for awhile.

"So what about my dad?" He looked up at her, puzzled.

Roberta explained to him that his father would be at the other house, but they would still see each other.

As he started exploring the house, he asked, "How do I get upstairs?"

His mother explained to him that this house did not have stairs, but he would still have his own room just like at his other house.

"I don't like this house. I like my other house better," he fussed.

"OK, let's go for now. We will come back another day when you are in a better mood," she told her son.

She still had so many things to pack and still did not have enough boxes. As she thought about packing she wondered how it would have been to take Chelsea along. She couldn't help wondering how the dog would have adjusted if they would even have been allowed to leave with her. Although still very sad about her passing, Roberta didn't have to worry about that now. Robyn no longer appeared upset about her passing as he rarely spoke about "my dog Chelsea" any more.

It's good the passing of the dog and the moving didn't coincide as the problem would have been severely compounded, thought Roberta.

It was such a challenge trying to do all that packing while still working. In just five days her dad and Angela would be flying over to be with her. She would be leaving her home soon.

Her mother-in-law called that same day to speak with her son, but Roberta answered the phone. She went from one topic to the other until she arrived at the fact that she and Robyn would be leaving in just days. She lamented the fact that Robyn shouldn't have to go through this, and as adults they should be able to work things out. She invited Roberta to her house as she claimed she much preferred a face-to-face encounter.

Roberta was instantly reminded of the day when she last went to Momsy's house. In spite of it all, she decided to see her mother-in-law just to hear her out. It was the very first time that they had talked at length since the uproar. Roberta was only planning on a short visit as she had an appointment set up with her lawyer regarding the divorce papers.

She had a timeline of couple more weeks to respond to the demands. All this time she had not discussed it, just trying to forget it. Since her mother-in-law initiated the meeting, Roberta decided to hold nothing back. She also knew Momsy was well aware of the situation.

It was heartrending to rehash the issues. They ranged from spousal support, to his attorney fees, to 50/50 child custody. There was no way Roberta was going to agree to any such terms and put her baby through that. She had no problems with Robyn's seeing his dad on weekends and holidays, but the to-and-fro during school and the instability were not going to happen. She was going to fight that with everything.

She had spent at least an hour and a half with her mother-in-law when Momsy decided to call her son up for a meeting. He arrived very solemnly and obviously in no mood for any discussion. Both Aubyn and Momsy explained that the demands made were for his protection in case Roberta was planning to make huge demands herself.

After one more hour with all three of them, Roberta and Aubyn left the discussion thinking that they would forget about the divorce and make another attempt to save the marriage. However, Aubyn's comment at the end of the meeting disturbed her. He made it abundantly clear that he was not going to cancel the paperwork, but rather would let it sit there just in case they agreed to follow through. He claimed he had no time to be redoing any paperwork. She could not see how someone who wanted to try again could be so pessimistic, but she went along with it anyway. She didn't think his whole heart was in it, but she thought it was still worth a try.

She was now faced with telling her dad and stepmom and feared her dad would be so angry since she was certain they would not be able to redeem much of their fare. She was right. After much sarcasm and being called a joker, she decided she would suffer the loss and compensate them.

The other task was to contact the owner of what was supposed to be her new home. The owner was quite upset and blamed her for allowing "good" people to pass up the home and leaving her without a tenant. The would-be landlady decided she would not be reimbursing her unless she found a tenant. Roberta knew she was at fault and apologized profusely. It was about one week later that the owner contacted her and informed her she would return to her the security deposit only.

Roberta had intensely mixed feeling. She was relieved things were patched up so at least Robyn would still be at his home. Her marriage was not close to what it should be, but she was sure they would be more careful and tolerant of each other, at least for a while.

Her dad stopped calling the house, but at least her stepmom called. She was truly a mom next to her own mom. Roberta had gone ahead and rerouted her check to their joint account and transferred all the money to it except for the money with which she had opened it.

Two months passed, and Roberta was routinely checking the account to ensure payments of bills and the status of the account. She noticed that two mortgage payments of similar amounts were withdrawn just days apart.

When she had changed to a separate account she was still writing him checks toward the mortgage and living expenses. She questioned the duplicate withdrawals, and he explained that he was behind by two months due to other expenses. It did not make any sense. She also noticed that their account was charged by a dating site for over $100.

Roberta was rather calm because by now she knew that her husband's lips were clamped shut if she did otherwise. She was bothered by the huge chunk that was deducted, but more so about the charges from the dating site. She had been leaving in January, but she didn't, and now in March a dating site? Everything was preposterous!

"Roberta, you never believe anything I say anyway, but that was from maybe close to two months ago. I will have to call them because I don't even know why they are charging me still, and I already cancelled. I did not even have any luck on the site."

He walked to the bathroom to take a shower, and she followed him still trying to understand the happenings. "Aubyn, do you realize I lost a lot of money by coming back into this relationship? I did anyway since saving the marriage to me is worth it," Roberta continued in a calm steady voice, which surprised even her.

"You always complained about money, and yet you had money to waste on a dating site. After all I have gone through, look at how stupid I appear to my own family by shoving my tail between my legs to return to you, practically a laughing stock."

With one leg already in the shower he turned the faucet on. "The decision for you to come back was between you and my mother. I had nothing to do with it."

It was undoubtedly a slap in the face. She was so humiliated and felt like a nobody. There was no way she could let her family hear this, not after everything. How could she live through this? This could not be the guy she thought was her soul mate. It felt she had been stabbed in the chest.

He continued, "Furthermore, my mom loves you like her own daughter and desperately wants things to work for us, and you don't even care for her. By the way, where is your gratitude, girl, after all she has done for us? Frankly, I am not going to choose anything over my family. I can get another wife, but not another mother!"

The insults really didn't get worse than that. She remembered advising a friend in a similar situation that she had to respect herself first, and if she were not getting respect, then it was time to go, and yet she was taking all these insults as an invitation!

Her simple response to him was, "You will not know what you have until you lose it, and you will be telling six more wives the same thing." She went into another room to sob. She decided that she wasn't going to let him see any more of her tears.

She could tell when he was sorry about something even when he did not apologize. When they had just gotten married "sorry" was an easy word for him. At least he did apologize about the dating site, whether he meant it or not. Lately too he had been offering to assist her when she was doing little tasks.

"Dear, I think we should try counseling again. I have been looking into it, and I can get it covered through my job. We could start as early as next week if you'd like," he told her.

"I think we should. Maybe someone out there can help," she agreed.

They went for four sessions. Each session was half an hour in duration. She actually liked the way the sessions were conducted. The counselor gave each of them an opportunity to speak. There was so much anger, and they both started to speak out of turn on multiple occasions. Aubyn was raising his voice quite often.

The counselor handed each of them a pointer when it was their turn to speak. When either tried to speak out of turn, he gestured to the pointer. Roberta actually liked the counselor's outlook on the situation. For the first time she was happy that someone saw things logically, and best of all it was a professional counselor chosen by Aubyn.

The counselor spoke about family boundaries and differentiated between immediate and extended family. He spoke about the different types of love as it related to spouses as opposed to parents and other family members. The importance of recreation with at least one family trip per year was also a controversial issue that Aubyn opposed vehemently. The job issue was also discussed as it related to the welfare and security of the family.

After the fourth meeting her husband refused to return claiming that he didn't see any benefit from the sessions. Roberta continued for two additional meetings by herself, but since the sessions were designed for both, there was no point in continuing.

Her dad only communicated with her via her cell phone or email, never by the house phone. She recalled his telling her that he guaranteed them just one year to be back to square one. She was doing everything to prove him wrong. She had to.

Roberta and Aubyn must have gotten something from those sessions because life was looking more normal. She had resolved not to be bothered by his going on his "second job" with nothing to show for it. He had told her previously that it was not fully worked out, and he was assisting the setup. He claimed that Thein would never cheat him, and he was not worried.

At least nowadays there was some improvement. He called whenever he was running late, which made a world of difference to her. Whenever he worked at his regular job, however, even though he got off before 7 am, she hardly saw him when she worked the morning shift. She left between 7 and 7:15 am for work, depending on where she was scheduled.

After not seeing her husband all night she hoped to see him at least before she left in the mornings. Several mornings as she left for work, she passed his van parked at his mom's house. However disappointing it was, she had learned not to say a word in order to maintain the peace.

Robyn was turning five on the July 12, but he had never been given a birthday party, although they always got him lots of gifts. Aubyn was not interested in having a party, and Roberta didn't worry about it.

The morning of his birthday, however, Roberta decided to have a few people over. She already had juices, ice cream, cones, and finger food at home. She just ran out and got a cake and some grilled chicken.

She called her mother-in-law first, explaining that it wasn't much of a party and nothing was planned. It was purely impromptu. She apologized for the short notice, but mentioned that she only thought of it that morning in order to make it more exciting for Robyn.

A total of seven people turned up. Robyn felt so important to have people over while he made a wish, blew out all five candles, and tried to cut his cake. As everyone got a plate and served themselves she heard her mother-in-law telling Aubyn that Roberta had planned Robyn's party knowing that Dean would be at work.

Roberta wanted to let her know that she heard the comment, but thought it might cause a scene and ignored it. She could not help wondering why she would even say that when the situation had been previously explained.

She tried to read the facial expressions and noticed that her mother-in-law did not appear pleased while her husband's was unreadable. Dean was typically easy-going, and she already planned to inform him that it was impromptu and to leave him a plate.

She anticipated some discussion regarding the same issue from her husband. She was quite sure that he would be annoyed with her. She was awaiting the famous words, "My mom said, or my mom complained." She listened for them, but nothing was said. As it turned out, that too bothered her because now she had no idea what he was thinking.

Several months went by, and all was well until October, just as her dad had predicted. Momsy had called the house. Roberta and she spoke for a while, and then she asked to speak with Aubyn. The telephone was on speaker phone when she gave her husband the phone, and he continued to speak with the speaker on for a few seconds. She noticed when he switched it from the speaker, but not before she heard his mom talk with him about a check.

Roberta was on the afternoon shift and had to rush out shortly. As she drove to work she was puzzled. Could he be turning in checks to his mom secretly while she was pouring everything into the joint account? She also recalled him talking to Thein just last week, and what he said then was adding up now.

She obviously couldn't hear what Thein was saying, but his response was enough to let her know that Thein was pleased with him. She heard when Aubyn said, "That's what you're paying me for, and you know a good man when you find one."

She drove to work that afternoon extremely bothered. Quite often while at work she pondered what she had heard. That evening when she got home, her mom was waiting up for her. "Phena gave me a message this evening for Aubyn, but he's been sleeping so you tell him for me."

Her mom relayed the message to her, and Roberta was furious. Everything made sense, and this time this was it. She was not going to be a fool any longer. She went straight to their bedroom, woke him, and delivered the message.

"Your mom called my mother and gave her a message for you because you were asleep. She said you shouldn't worry about the check that you gave her to keep that got misplaced. She is sure she will find it just the same way she found the previous one that was lost."

"Oh, thanks," he said, his eyes red from just waking up.

She asked him to explain about these checks, hoping there was some reasonable explanation.

"I have nothing to say. You are going to think whatever you feel anyway, so there is no point for me to even attempt to explain," he answered sternly.

His attitude only confirmed what she initially thought. He made no effort to defend himself or to clarify. It was clear that he didn't care how she felt or what she was going through.

"We are going to the bank tomorrow. I want half of what is in the account. I have been dumping all I have into it while you have been putting away money. This is done, over. Do you understand? I want out!"

After the money was split, Roberta contacted her lawyer and began the process of responding to the divorce. She went to her realtor, and the house hunting began again.

That very day her agent showed her one on her office computer that had just posted the previous day. It was on the same street as the previous one, but had a nicer backyard which was a plus. This time it was a two-level house, so she hoped Robyn would like it.

The paperwork was quickly processed. She was one of the first applicants, and she was approved in just four days. The same payment was required as last time, and as she pulled out the check book to write the check for $3,000, she could not stop the tears.

The realtor was a religious person, and she offered words of comfort. As she was comforted, she couldn't help blurting out, "How is he going to manage with the mortgage and the property tax? They are about due now. This money should be going to help him and not going to pay someone else. I don't know how he is going to manage."

Roberta's mom had gone home to the Caribbean on a preplanned trip that could not be reversed, so she would not be around to assist with the packing. She definitely was not expecting her parents in Florida to fly over, but they came, sure enough. They arrived on November 1, 2011. All the utilities were turned on, but there was no refrigerator and no washer or dryer.

Roberta would not be moving in until she got a day off, which would be November 3. Aubyn had moved Robyn's bedroom set down to the house as well a single sofa and a television set. She had asked for the bedroom set in the downstairs guest room, the refrigerator, and washer and dryer, but was told she could not have them until the divorce was final. Roberta had no choice but to purchase all these things on credit. Emotionally she was a wreck, and the support from her parents was without measure.

CHAPTER 16:
THE UNBELIEVABLE

Roberta still had some books and some kitchen utensils left at Sweden Estates, so she called Aubyn to let him know she would be stopping by. She was accompanied by her stepmom Angela. She was so glad her stepmom decided to accompany her because she hadn't realized just how many books she had left behind. Angela also noticed the cushion that she had given them with a gorgeous picture of both of them imprinted on it and packed it as well.

Roberta divided the kitchen utensils equally, even splitting some of her own in two. His mom had given them two sauce pans, and Roberta decided to take one. She abruptly halted when he reminded her, "That was given to me by my mom."

"Aubyn, it was given to us. I don't have any, and that's why I was taking this one," she said.

"I don't plan on replacing anything, and if you take it, that's what I will have to do," he told her.

"You know what, it's OK. Take it if you're going to be so exact! What's the difference one pot is going to make? I still have to buy everything else anyway."

Roberta was through and just about to leave when she decided to reconfirm the drop off and pickup of Robyn for school that week. She would be able to transport him for three days as she would be working the evening shift those days. She needed his assistance for the remaining two days. This would be the first week that Robyn would be traveling from another location to school.

"I have absolutely no problem with transporting my son with regards to school, but after school he's staying here until you come get him," he said roughly.

"You know that's not possible when I am on the evening shift. I would not be home until after 10 pm, so you expect me to get him then when he should be asleep?"

"I have to rely on my mom to assist with that when I am not able, and my mom and I will not be into the back and forth. I can assure you of that!"

Roberta was transfixed for a moment. Surely that was not much to ask, and he had to make it a big deal. *Why?* she asked silently.

"My mom, my mom, everything my mom! Can't you quit that for a second?" she scoffed.

He rolled his big full eyes and looked at her. If looks could kill she probably would be dead.

"See the attitude? You need to be by yourself. You shouldn't be with anyone!" he shouted.

"Don't worry about me. That is surely going to be your fate, just wait and see!" she yelled back at him. "Think about it. You are on the night-shift, and your mom is busy most of the day. Can't you see that?"

They had previously discussed that whenever Roberta was on the morning shift Aubyn would pick his son up from school. Robyn would stay at his dad's house, that way he would spend time with his dad, and she would get him on her way from work. She also told him that whenever he wanted to spend time with their son just to give her adequate notice.

Her mom would return at the end of November, but for now her other parents were here to support her and assist with Robyn. The most feasible thing to do, therefore, was to leave their son at her house when she worked the late shift where he would be attended to.

The first day she returned to work after she moved from the only place she truly knew as home, reality hit her really hard. She managed to escape into the bathroom for a brief few minutes and let it all out unbeknownst to anyone. It was strange, but as busy as she was at work, these emotions seemed to envelop her more while on the job.

That evening while returning from work, she took the wrong turn, not remembering that route no longer led home. Fortunately she only needed to drive an additional ten minutes to correct the error.

It was amazing how much Angela and her dad got done while she was at work. Each day the house seemed more like home. Aubyn allowed her to bring Robyn's computer with her. She did not get a desk for it, so it was placed on the floor. Roberta had no idea when she was going to be able to get him one with everything else she had ahead of her. However, one evening she got home and noticed his computer was no longer on the floor.

"Where did you guys get this desk?" she asked her stepmom and dad. "It's nice and neat. How much do I owe you for this?"

"We realized that Robyn needed one, and we just saw what we've been looking for," said her stepmom with a smile. "And you owe us nothing."

Robyn was dropped off by his dad and was given a bath and fed by her stepmom. She thought in spite of everything how blessed she truly was because with her job and schedule there was just no way she could handle this alone.

As the weeks went by there were so many demands made by the attorneys. She was required to produce stacks and stacks of paperwork as the ugly battle proceeded. Many nights after work she was up for several hours making copies of pertinent documents.

There was always an appointment; there were mediation dates and court hearings. Roberta wished it would all just go away. She didn't want to fight. She didn't want it to be unpleasant. All she wanted was for them to come to an agreement, and she would just walk away.

Aubyn and Roberta had become such strangers, it was tearing her up inside. They only spoke as it related to Robyn, and that was mainly communicated via email or pager.

Angela and her dad had returned home the day after her mom returned, as planned. She believed it was the saddest Christmas she had every spent in all her thirty-six years. Roberta met with her attorney after the holiday to convey to the opposing counsel that she would walk away from everything if the demands were dropped.

Roberta knew she was entitled to half of his retirement, the house, and its contents as well as other assets. If he dropped the spousal support, 50/50 custody, and coverage of attorney fees, she would drop her counter requests.

Several weeks went by, and no response was forthcoming. Robyn had settled down into his new home and was adjusting quite well and was even more elated that his grandma had returned. There was one other issue: he couldn't understand why Grandma Angela and Grandpa had to return to Florida.

Roberta knew she had to speak with Aubyn and soon. He had not been seeing Robyn except for the brief moments when he assisted with transporting him to and from school. This was affecting Robyn as lately he has been complaining of missing his dad and had been asking deep questions.

"Mommy, why do we have to have two homes? I only want one home so I can see you and my dad," said Robyn.

"I know, baby, but no matter what happens, I love you, and your daddy loves you, and you will always have both of us," she told him.

"Mommy why did my dad chase you out of our house? Is it because you argue with him too much?" asked Robyn.

"Robyn, no one chased anyone out, and yes, we were not getting along so we decided to be apart, but that will never change anything where you are concerned. Do you understand that?"

He shrugged his shoulders in response and ran off saying he was going to watch *Caillou*, one of his favorite cartoons.

At this point she really had to have a talk with his dad. Regardless of the separation and whatever else had changed, she wanted their son to know that their love and commitment to him had not and would not change.

She did get a hold of him, but he appeared quite preoccupied as his tone was hasty and uninviting. He told her he would call her back. He called her later that evening. She gave him the option to talk over the phone or schedule a time where they both could meet with Robyn. He flatly told her that he was quite busy, and his schedule was unpredictable, so the phone would have to do.

Although Robyn liked the backyard with the beautiful landscape and the basketball court, at least once per week he complained of missing his dad. When Roberta was off from work, she allowed him to drive his little car in the garage or ride his bike, but she was only Mommy, not both Mommy and Daddy. His grandma would occasionally take him in the backyard to kick a ball as well, but that did not totally console him.

Sometimes she sat and reflected in her bedroom, and as her mind drifted off, quite often her son entered the room unannounced. "What are you doing, Mommy? I love you, Mommy."

She heard the, "I love you, Mommy," several times per day. It gave her life new meaning. She was never short of compliments. When she dressed even for a quick run to the grocery store she heard, "Mommy, I like your dress. Mommy, you look so nice." Truly he inspired her, and when she thought to question the Almighty, she was reminded that he blessed her with Robyn.

The end of the marriage was well on its way. It was already January 2012, and she was still having a difficult time accepting everything. She wished she could go to sleep, wake up, and tell her son it was a bad dream.

One night Roberta had a panic attack as the stress of it all just rested on her. She felt claustrophobic, and she had difficulty breathing. For several years she had occasionally had problems breathing depending on the climate, but she was sure this was triggered by her current circumstances.

Her mom, being a light sleeper, heard her as she jumped out of bed looking for her inhaler and rushed over to assist her. She quickly used the inhaler and some other remedies her mom concocted. However, mom talking with her and reassuring her was more therapeutic than the inhaler.

Realizing that she was in need of professional counseling to get through the ordeal, especially where it pertained to how she related to Robyn, she thought of Pastor Don. Roberta called him the following day, and an appointment was made for the afternoon after work. She felt confident that she was led to him by divine intervention as he had performed her premarital counseling. He also was one of the three officiating ministers at their wedding.

In the first meeting he had asked for an overview of the situation. She gave him a synopsis to which he expressed deep regret. His approach was one of urgency as she outlined the dates of the hearings. The first hearing was scheduled for the latter part of January, while the others were the first and last weeks of February. The initial meeting was a status meeting, and therefore only the attorneys were required to attend.

"I want to help with this real bad," he told her. "But my hands can't be tied. I have to do this according to how I am led."

The meeting commenced with prayer, for which she was truly thankful. Pastor Don was hoping he could have a meeting with Aubyn individually, after which he would schedule a meeting with both parties. Roberta left the meeting fired up with hope.

The following day Roberta stopped at Sweden Estates after leaving work to pick up her son. Aubyn was more than cordial to her, even asking her how her day went. He told her some mail was there for her and gestured for her to go inside for it. She had not been inside the house in about two months, but it was still the familiar home. Everything was basically the same.

She was impressed to smell food. She couldn't help but ask what was for dinner. He told her he did some stir-fry vegetables with chicken. He asked her if she wanted to try it. It was attractive the orange color from the carrots contrasted well with the green vegetables, and it was good. He never cooked an entire meal while she was there, although he had stuffed and roasted a chicken once. She had taken a picture of it for fear that would be his last attempt.

He had challenged her many times, "Just leave me the ingredients, and I will cook." Now she was sorry she hadn't taken him up on that offer because he did do a good job. She noticed his laptop down stairs, and as he rebooted she noticed how slow it was.

The very first laptop she owned had been given to her by him, and she still held it dear. He looked a little frustrated, and she knew how much it meant to him. It was not only his job, but also his hobby. She had always wanted to surprise him with one.

When she had gotten the small check from her insurance policy overseas, she desperately wanted to surprise him with a new laptop. She knew he would complain that they couldn't afford it, but she would have anyway. Unfortunately there was a major falling out between them at that time, and it did not materialize.

She watched him as it slowly booted up and wished she could make him happy as she had been when she received her own. Roberta left that evening thinking she would purchase one on her credit card and surprise him.

As she thought about incurring the extra expense, she wondered if she were crazy for doing this. He might not even accept it. Two days later she was on the early shift; she left work and went to purchase a Toshiba laptop for him. It was the same brand he had gotten her so many years before.

Her heart raced as she called to let him know she was outside to get Robyn. She told him she had a laptop that she wanted him to look at to ensure it had the latest updates. As he gently held it and looked at it he said, "Nice machine, no problem. I will look at it for you. How soon will you need it?"

She could hold it no longer, so she told him it was his and explained for so long she had wanted to do this. She was relieved that he accepted it. As he bent down to embrace her, he was overcome by emotions.

"I really needed it. You just don't know how much...but you really didn't have to."

"I know you needed one for a long time, and now you finally have one."

"Thank you, dear, this is indeed a surprise. It is really neat. I like it, and this model has lots more capabilities than my old one. Thanks."

The following week she had a second session with Pastor Don, still feeling the need to obtain counsel. She wasn't sure if he attempted to contact Aubyn as he didn't mention it. She figured if that were so, he would have told her. The meeting once again was therapeutic. As usual she was allowed to speak, after which he gave counsel that generally alluded to scriptures concerning marriage.

The third meeting occurred in February just about five days before mediation. This time the meeting was somewhat shorter, but once again concluded on a high note. He claimed he would break one of the rules of marriage counseling by trying to reach her mother-in-law to get in touch with her son. He said he would be contacting her that same evening after the counseling session.

Roberta had mixed feelings about that sort of approach, but agreed any way. Just before she left, he told her they could follow up the following day at 5:15 pm. Roberta tried calling him when she left work as she normally did to ensure the meeting was still on, but got no response. She drove to his office nonetheless and called again, but no response. She even left voice messages that she had stopped by, but he did not return her call.

As she drove home she figured Pastor Don had an unexpected meeting and would contact her to reschedule. The rest of February went by, and he never contacted Roberta. She felt as if she just unveiled her whole life's story just for his information and was left hanging. She wondered if she would ever know what really happened, but she never made contact with Pastor Don as he had never returned any of her calls.

Aubyn called her one day. She expected it to be the usual call about Robyn, but this time it was regarding a settlement. He wanted to know exactly what she wanted, and he decided to communicate with her directly as they were currently on speaking terms.

"I want nothing as long as you drop the request for alimony and child custody as well as pay your attorney fees. I will be fine with everything else," she told him.

"Are you sure? What about my retirement and the stuff in the house? Because remember when this is settled, that's it."

"Well, in terms of child care, I notice that there is no stipulated amount, plus—"

"Like I said, I will drop all of what you requested, but I'm sorry I cannot specify an amount. As it is I am stuck with the mortgage by myself, and I just have too much to take care of," interrupted Aubyn.

"It didn't have to get to this, but it is what it is. As I was trying to say earlier, there are a couple other changes that have to be made on the document."

"Yes, like what?"

"You want me to sign my rights off Sweden Estates, but not the other place in short sale to which I have absolutely no attachment. How fair is that?"

By the time she left they had come to an agreement, and it was a pleasant surprise that voices were kept at a normal pitch. Roberta did not want the hassle or the prolonged court appearances. As far as she was concerned the sooner this was settled the better because truly she felt couldn't handle much more.

It took two long weeks before the revised papers were returned to her attorney. Roberta signed the final papers on February 16 that drew the curtain down on her marriage. It was a dark day for her, and it seemed like her wedding day flashed right before her. This was not happening.

It was only two days earlier that he had called to wish her happy Valentine's Day, perhaps for old time's sake. She didn't expect it, but for some strange reason was happy he did. They even shared a meal together at his home when she came to pick up Robyn on her way from work.

In just a matter of time they would be strangers again as though they had never met. She didn't know if he had already signed his papers, but probably he had. February 23 came, and she received calls and cards from friends and relatives.

She couldn't recall ever being scheduled off from work on her birthday, but for whatever reason she was off that day and the two following. Roberta had been considering purchasing a new car since the previous year. The mileage on her car was very high, and the front end was smashed pretty badly on her way to work one day as the car skidded on black ice.

Her job required her to float to various locations according to the need, and, unfortunately, she was sent to work in the mountains at elevations of around 7,000 feet where it frequently snowed.

She did not see the ice, the car skidded, and the only way she knew to stop it was to slam it into the hillside.

Aubyn used to tell her that they didn't need to be making car payments. Not that it mattered now, but he changed his tune somewhat when he saw the damage. She had made up her mind just the week preceding her birthday that she would treat herself to a new car for her birthday.

If her dad were close by, she would definitely ask him to accompany her on the purchase. She really had no one else to ask but Aubyn, whom she felt was knowledgeable about cars. He told her it was no problem, but he wouldn't be available until late afternoon.

Each time the phone rang she thought it might be him then chided herself for acting like a giddy teenager. It was silly, and she knew it. The divorce would be final any day now, but she still hoped he would call to wish her a happy birthday.

He was the third person to call, and usually he would have been the first to wish her happy birthday. She smiled at the memory. He also reconfirmed the late afternoon appointment for the car dealership.

It was a relief having a male figure there with her as she was clueless about automobiles. He examined and inspected every detail, and he test drove the car. It was ironic that most of the discussion was directed to him. The salesperson explained that he was showing Mr. Sullivan how to operate the different features as he was sure he would be doing that for his wife. He looked like the perfect husband, and he played the part so well.

Roberta was a little timid to drive the car at first. It was bigger than her other car and had so many gadgets. She wondered when she would learn all the features and suddenly felt sad when she realized he wasn't going to be there to help her with it. At least he was sitting next to her as she drove it home.

He told her that if she had time they could watch a couple of movies together since it was her birthday, and he would be free for the rest of the evening. It felt like old times, and, oh, how she missed this. They had barely finished watching one of them when it was getting dark outside.

"I really would like to watch the second one, but it's late already. The only way would be if I could go get some stuff at home and spend the night here in another room."

"Sure that's fine with me. We could drive down for your stuff, and that way we could enjoy the other movie."

The second movie was a combination of family and mystery. There was much suspense, and there were some scenes that proved scary. It didn't help that he watched movies in utter darkness. He knew her well enough after all the years that she wasn't into much of the scary stuff. He soon assured her that there were very few scenes like that, and he drew closer to her just as if they were still a couple.

She had a good birthday. She was not going to think about tomorrow; she only wanted to enjoy her day. The movie was all done, and it was time for bed, and like the gentleman she knew in former years, he offered her a hot drink and a choice of what to eat. Where did it all go wrong? Why did it come to this when she still loved him and when she took those vows she meant forever? He never said it but she believed he still must care for her too.

She went upstairs to gather her things to head to another room when he told her, "You can stay in this room, dear. I'll just stay on my side. This was your room too, remember?"

It was with mixed feelings she decided to stay in what used to be their bedroom. She lay there with her back turned to him when she felt his arms encircling her shoulders. It must have been instinct because she didn't think twice as she snuggled close to him. It didn't feel wrong. After all, it wasn't final as yet. She still had not received the final document. Maybe he still had not signed.

Nothing was planned. She did not plan to sleep over. It all happened spontaneously because of the movie. As she rolled over to see daylight, she was reminded instantly it was February 24, his birthday. She was definitely the first to wish him happy birthday, and how interesting, whether by fate or whatever else, her new car spent its very first night at Sweden Estates.

In spite of the circumstances, she had enjoyed her birthday. She was pensive whenever she was not occupied by him, but at least that day she was not sad. Roberta was generally expressive and had to say what was on her mind, which was not always a good idea.

She had awoken early as she had to get home to get Robyn to school.

"Aubyn, thanks for yesterday. Thanks for making it a special birthday. It meant a lot to me, and I'm glad I could at least start yours with you. Oh, by the way, Robyn and I got you something. Let me go grab it."

She ran downstairs and got it for him. He said thanks, but didn't open it right away.

"I haven't told you this in a long time, but I love you, and all we've been through hasn't changed that," she told him.

He didn't say he loved her instead he proceeded with another response. "I hear you, I… hear you. Sometimes I reflect on the past also, but we are not making it Roberta. It's too much work, heavens know we've tried."

"Are you so quick to throw it all away?" Roberta asked. "I'm sure your mom, or your brother, or some other relative at some point truly upset you to the point where you are livid. It happens to everyone."

"Yes, and?"

"Our relatives get us upset, and we can't divorce them. They are still family, so why should we look at marriage as disposable, something that is so sacred and ordained by God, as of less importance? Aubyn, tell me why."

She had no intention of letting him see her cry, but her voice cracked, and she struggled to fight back the tears. "We've both been hurt, you and me, and yet I still think we can do something to fix this. I mean, I didn't see us as being part of the statistics. I value commitment, and I meant every word I said eight and a half years ago. Didn't you?"

"Roberta, you know I did. Please, I don't want you crying. I don't like that. Who knows why we are apart. It's a time for reflection. Remember too, I didn't want this. You were the one threatening me all these years with a divorce," he told her.

"I have to go now. I don't want to be late," she said as she walked toward the bedroom door.

"I hardly ever say anything because it is usually taken the wrong way, but while we are apart, let's take it as a break. Let's meet other people and see what happens. I never really dated. Who knows? Maybe the right person is out there for you or for me," said Aubyn.

"You have made it clear. You don't have to say more; it is indeed done," she acknowledged.

"See, that's why I don't say anything. I'm only saying let's meet other people. We haven't even been separated for six months. Let's take a break. Who knows? If we get divorced and it is ordained for us to reunite, we could remarry. I honestly believe now is the time for soul searching."

"OK, I will never initiate this discussion again. I have to realize that we are no longer a couple and just move on. Marriage was not meant for everyone. I really have to go now."

He walked her down the stairs, and as she reversed from the garage she could see that he was in no hurry to shut it.

It was only ten minutes to get home, and she had to look normal by the time she got there. Hopefully, her eyes weren't red from the crying since she didn't want either Robyn or her mom to be worried.

She felt cheap. She felt as though she were chasing after him when he obviously had another agenda. All her life she never did that, and now she was.

When she got home, her mom had already dressed Robyn. Roberta rushed him to school, and he arrived just before the first bell rang. Although she was still on a day off, she had a busy day ahead, and thankfully she would not have time to think about her own problems.

It was already April 4. She hadn't seen Aubyn in over a month. She was still at home. She had not yet left for the afternoon shift. He called her home to tell her he was outside because he had some mail from the house for her. He looked so thin. It hurt to see how much weight he had lost apparently from running between jobs and not sparing enough time to eat or sleep. Nevertheless, he seemed to be in a great mood. He was almost grinning when he saw her.

Later, she sent him an email: *Please take care of yourself. I know you're busy, but you must make time to EAT, SLEEP and PRAY, praying for you… love u still.*

As an afterthought she regretted saying so much. Roberta didn't realize that she really still cared so deeply until that feeling overtook her when he stopped by looking so tired and drawn.

She was not expecting a response because many previous emails had been ignored. She received a speedy but simple response that read: *Thanks, dear, appreciate it.*

Roberta impulsively decided to give him a quick call. "I meant what I said in the email. Please take care of yourself, and I do love you still."

There was a pregnant pause on the other end then he quietly spelt the word "L-O-V-E." Since the separation she must have told him at least four times, and this was the first he ever did. He didn't really tell her, though, he spelled it.

The very next day she was on the evening shift again. She had to pick up her son by 11:50 am then head to work. Roberta decided to stop by the alternative mailbox just before picking up Robyn from school. There were surprisingly quite a few pieces of mail, but there was a large brown envelope that caught her attention. She immediately recognized it; it was from her lawyer.

As she opened it she saw *Judgment* stamped with a sign-off date of March 28. As she looked further she noticed that he had signed on February 23. She had signed hers two days after Valentine Day. He signed on her birthday, and the judgment was final on her younger brother's birthday.

In one sense she felt relieved that there would be no more surprises and no more demands from the opposing counsel, and the other feeling she realized was that 7/6/03 was no longer significant. She didn't cry, and Robyn had no idea that something so important had just occurred in their lives when she got him from school.

She dropped Robyn off and spared enough time to inform her mom that it was indeed final, and then she turned up the hill for work. As she drove to work she couldn't help wondering if the reason for Aubyn's grin were his receipt of the final judgment.

The ride to work was not long enough. She just wanted time to think about life and the reality that it was truly over. She was now a single parent. How would she tell Robyn that no hope was left for reconciliation? He was too young to understand, so she would keep it simple. All he needed to know was that they both loved him and that he should not worry about anything else.

In spite of herself, over and over the song, that she sang in the past that had no meaning to her, suddenly did. Tammy Wynette singing, *The D-I-V-O-R-C-E becomes final today and me and little J-O-E will be going away*. Roberta was proud of herself that she was no longer bitter; neither did she have any resentment, although she felt disappointment and sadness. She had prayed so hard for peace, and she believed it had been granted. Despite the peace however, Roberta was left with the ever present pain, somewhat reduced to a dull gnawing ache.

The Hill View pastor being cognizant of the perils that plague many marriages often builds his sermon around marriage and the family. Parts of his sermons seemed to replay in her head more frequently but they were soothing.

He borrowed words from one of her favorite religious writers, E.G. White, "Divorce is a lifelong heartfelt sore." He continued to quote her "it is a violent dismemberment of the one flesh marriage." Those words captured it all. She had felt so many things but no other words hit the nail on the head quite like that. It was indeed a sore that wasn't healing and she was dismembered.

In spite of everything it was amazing to see how amicable everyone was with each other. Her ex-mother-in-law called her mother, and her mother called her in return. Roberta and Aubyn basically spoke only as s it pertained to their son, and they were civil.

It was, however, an unfortunate day that brought that to a sudden end. Roberta was on the morning shift and so had to be at her job by 8 am. Robyn had to be at school before 8 am, and as usual on such days a prior arrangement had been made with his dad. Roberta both tele-phoned him as well as sent him a reminder by email.

Roberta received a troubling call from her mom saying that it was 7:55 am and Aubyn had not shown up. She was at work and there was no way she could help, and by the tone of her mom's voice she knew she was going to explode. She feared it could get ugly. Her mom ended the conversation by stating that she was going to call Phena right now to locate her son.

It was ten minutes later that Roberta's cell phone rang, and it was her mom. She was talking so loudly and rapidly that she had a hard time understanding her. She managed to get her to calm down when the story unfolded.

She said Phena was rather annoyed, stating that her son had a lot on him, and if he were late there was no need for any alarm and there had to be a logical explanation. Dims proceeded to inform her that she really didn't care about anything except Robyn's arriving at school on time, which was already impossible.

Both women accused each other of being instrumental in the breakup of their children's marriage, and harsh words were exchanged. Momsy blamed her mom for not making peace while she lived with Aubyn and Roberta, while her mom accused her of trying to control their lives from the very start.

Momsy had not called the house in over a week, which was not typi-cal. They generally talked once or twice a week on average. The phone rang around 8 am on Sunday morning, and it was she. Roberta answered the phone, "Hello, how is it going?"

"You wouldn't want to know, girl. I am so tired, and I didn't sleep well last night with so much on my mind," said her mother-in-law.

"You still have to take it easy, and you have to rest," Roberta encouraged.

"I wonder why things happen in life, but they do for a reason. I know I've been misunderstood, and all I have done was out of love. You are the daughter I never had, Roberta. Everyone makes mistakes. I'd like to see one who doesn't."

"Yep, we all do." Roberta took a deep breath.

"The important thing is that we learn from it, and God sees and knows, and He can fix everything," said Momsy.

"I used to question the Lord also, but like you said, all things happen for a reason, and I do believe it is to make us better. Who knows? Our experience may enrich someone else's life," Roberta stated pensively.

Roberta didn't tell her, but one of her friends was having serious marital issues, and her own experience was a source of support and encouragement to her friend. In fact, her friend's outlook had changed for the better, and she had seen some improvement in her marriage.

The air was all tense again between her mom and mother-in-law, and Roberta regretted it. Enough had already occurred; she just needed peace. She knew her mom would snap out of it, but it would be a while.

She could not comprehend why Aubyn was late. Her mom told her he eventually turned up to get Robyn at 8 am, and that this was not the first time he had been so late.

Roberta decided she had to talk with him as this could go against their child at school. She would not speak with him until she knew she was calm enough to do so. She did not get the opportunity to speak to him for several days. She sent him several emails, but when he finally responded he told her that he had been extremely busy as he had been receiving multiple calls from clients.

It was rather strange, but he was in no apparent haste to end the call when he telephoned Roberta. He was more than civil and surprisingly showed interest in how her day was spent.

For what it was worth, his priorities seemed to have switched some-what. She no longer heard him expressing interest in meeting other women, and he informed her that he had unsubscribed from most of the online sites that bothered her. Recently, he alluded to being the "prodi-gal," and it did seem like he wanted to return home.

She was overjoyed when he expressed desire to be fully back in the church. Roberta could not believe she was actually hearing these words. "I am elated to hear you speak so positively and with such confidence," Roberta told him.

"I decided it wasn't worth it going on those sites because the next person will not understand or if by some miracle we go back…"

Roberta did not hear the rest of the statement. The divorce had been final at least six weeks ago. How she would have been elated to hear this speech before the end. As she pondered on all that had transpired Roberta knew she had done all that was humanly possible to save her marriage. She also knew that there is nothing in a marital relationship that cannot be fixed but not of one's self but only through the power of The Most High.

Why couldn't Aubyn have said all this before? Why? All those days while driving or passing some arbitrary place, she would be a tearful mess when she heard certain music. One that evoked intense emotion was the song by Bill Withers, "Just the Two of Us."

That song had such meaning; it was one of the few handpicked for their wedding reception. All those times while they were apart, she had selected it as a soundtrack for her laptop. It played each time her computer started as well as with her screensaver. It never failed to bring on a flood of memories. Lately, she no longer cried when it played, but the memories were her faithful companions.

She was contented in the thought, and still believed one should never give up on one's marriage until trying all one possibly could, and that she knew she did. The path their lives would take from this point on was in the hands of the Almighty.